WORLD WAR TWO
MILITARY VEHICLES
TRANSPORT & HALFTRACKS

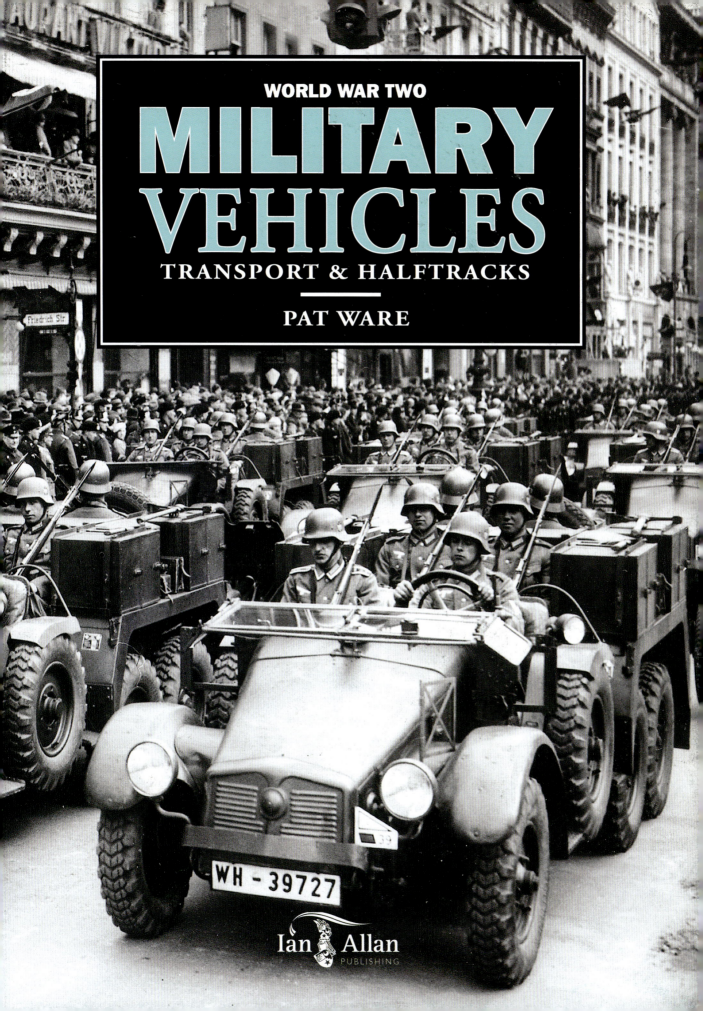

WORLD WAR TWO

MILITARY VEHICLES

TRANSPORT & HALFTRACKS

PAT WARE

WH - 39727

Ian Allan
PUBLISHING

Acknowledgements

This book could not have been produced without the help, expertise and encouragement over the years of David Fletcher, Librarian at the Tank Museum, Bovington, *(TM)* and their photographer Roland Groom *(RG/TM)*; Andrew Renwick of the Royal Air Force Museum *(RAFM)*; Brian S Baxter of the REME Museum; staff at the Imperial War Museum *(IWM)*; the archive of Ullstein Bild *(UB)*; US National Archives *(USNa)*; 303rd Bomber Group Foundation, Michael Faley *(303rdbg)*; Thomas Anderson *(An)*; and, of course, the late Bart Vanderveen. Thanks also to the Tank Museum for sourcing many original documents, photographs, prints and drawings; and to Phillip Royal *(PR)*, and Simon Thomson *(ST)* for their superb colour photographs.

Jasper Spencer-Smith
Bournemouth, England
July 2007

Conceived and edited by Jasper Spencer-Smith
Design editor: Nigel Pell
Jacket Design: Crispin Goodall
Scanning: JPS Ltd, Branksome, Poole, BH12 1DJ
Produced by JSS Publishing Limited,
P.O. Box 6031, Bournemouth, BH1 9AT, England

First published 2007

ISBN   978 0 7110 3193 2

Published by Ian Allan Publishing

An imprint of Ian Allan Publishing Ltd, Hersham, Surrey KT12 4RG

Printed by Ian Allan Printing Ltd, Hersham, Surrey KT12 4RG

Code: 0707/C

Visit the Ian Allan Publishing website at www.ianallanpublishing.com

Title spread: A parade in Berlin of *Wehrmacht* mechanised anti-tank gun unit in Krupp L2H43 6x4 light trucks. The occasion is to celebrate the 47th birthday of Adolf Hitler, 20 April 1936. *(UB)*

Contents

Introduction

It could be argued convincingly that the state of readiness with which each of the three major combatants - Britain, Germany and the USA - entered World War Two reflected their different national characters. Germany had been preparing for war since the mid-1930's whilst Britain had spent little on re-armament during that period, hoping that a major conflict could be avoided. The USA believed that Europe should sort out its own problems and that it was all too far away to be of any concern... isolationism was considered to be the best policy.

But things don't always go according to plan.

As it happened, through a combination of luck, ingenuity and hard work, and notwith-standing the odd disaster, Britain managed to produce the trucks, armoured fighting vehicles - also, of course aircraft and ships - to hold off Hitler's war machine long enough for help to arrive from the other side of the Atlantic. And, when the USA finally realised that the war in Europe really was a global affair, that nation's massive industrial production capacity rightly earned it the title of the "arsenal of democracy". Curiously, Germany was hoist on its own petard, producing military vehicles which were technically superior but which were complex and difficult to build in sufficient numbers. It is a paradox that the nation that invented the concept of mechanised *Blitzkrieg* entered World War 2, at least partially, dependent on horse-drawn transport, mounted troops, and a multiplicity of civilian vehicles.

Nevertheless, there is little doubt that the six-year conflict that we describe as World War Two was an incredible hothouse for automotive innovation and that this had an enormous effect on the design of military vehicles. Certainly for Britain and the USA there was little comparison between the vehicles that were in service at the beginning of the conflict and those which were being produced in 1945.

But wars are not only fought by the men with guns in their hands, and each nation understood that standardisation was the key to maximising production capacity even if the achievement of the goal proved difficult.

For example, there is a tendency, rightly, to think that Britain took whatever it could get from the domestic motor industry, with little standardisation between the products of different manufacturers. The result was that many vehicles were far from satisfactory.

It is also considered that the USA was more successful in standardising on a small number of specialised military vehicles, concentrating on turning these out in large numbers. Whilst there is some truth to this view, there is also a tendency to be influenced by the vehicles that have survived to the present day. Alongside the standardised Jeeps, Jimmys, Chevrolets, Diamond Ts and Dodges, there were many less well-known machines which played their part in the conflict but which were produced in small numbers by companies which have subsequently disappeared. Few enthusiasts these days are familiar with the products of companies such as Available, Hug, Biederman, Thew, Hendrickson, Walter, Sterling and Corbitt, and yet the contract records show that these organisations supplied trucks to the US Army, sometimes in small numbers, but nevertheless all played their part in the final victory.

Canada certainly showed the best grasp of the significance of standardisation, but perhaps with just three domestic manufacturers this should be no surprise. The standardised Canadian Military Pattern (CMP) machines combined technical competence with ease of production and might be considered to have established a pattern for the design of military machinery in the post-war years.

Germany was a different matter altogether.

Above: Typical of the US approach to the standardisation of military vehicles is the WC series Dodge. There were five versions of the $^3/_4$-ton 4x4 chassis, including a weapons carrier, ambulance, command car, carryall and maintenance vehicles; there was also this 1$^1/_2$-ton 6x6 variant which shared some 90% of components. *(RG/TM)*

Left: The speed of the Allied advance created considerable logistical and supply problems. Although the 2$^1/_2$-ton GMC was the US Army's standard supply vehicle, larger trucks were also employed in an attempt to keep the advancing troops supplied. Typical of these is the International Harvester M425/M426 tractor designed for use with 10-ton semi-trailers. *(RG/TM)*

Right: The *Blitzkrieg* concept called for logistical vehicles which would be able to keep up with the Panzer troops; this required speed and off-road ability. In the foreground, a typical medium off-road personnel carrier is parked up alongside two PzKpfw II light tanks. Behind this is a 3-ton Opel Blitz, and a typical 6x4 or 6x6 medium truck. *(UB)*

Re-armament had started in earnest with Hitler's coming to power in 1933, and spending rose accordingly, from perhaps five million *Reichmarks* in 1933 to 11 million in 1934, with every motor manufacturer encouraged to virtually do his own thing. By the middle of the decade, there was such a multiplicity of vehicle types in service that specifications were laid down in an attempt to standardise vehicles into six categories – light, medium and heavy personnel carriers, and light, medium and heavy trucks, all with two- and four-wheel drive, and a few also with four-wheel steering. But three years later, the range of vehicles in use was still such that further steps were required to reduce it further. The Schell Plan of 1938 attempted to reduce the number of truck types from more than 100 to less than 20, and the number of cars from 55 to 30; the emphasis was on standardised chassis, which could be combined with standardised body types to provide a vehicle which was suited to a particular role. But Germany still entered the war with far too many different types of vehicle and with an obsession with technical competence that slowed production... by the time this was abandoned, it was probably too late to affect the outcome of the war.

This book, then, is an attempt to summarise the multiplicity of military vehicles used by all of the major players during the long years of war. The approach that has been adopted breaks the vehicles down by type and then by country of origin. It includes many of the vehicles from the mid- to late-1930s which were available in 1939/40 – although it is impossible to know for sure exactly what remained in service – as well as those which were designed and produced as the war progressed.

The text describes significant or innovative machines, whilst the tables attempt to list all of the vehicles available for the particular role, giving a standardised nomenclature and basic descriptive and technical information. Dates given are generally for the introduction of the chassis type; specific dates are only given for the introduction of the particular vehicle where known. It is interesting how the tables show the dependency of Italy and Germany on diesel engines for larger vehicles, whilst the USA clearly preferred gasoline, even if this meant employing engines of massive displacement.

It is not possible to claim that the tables are 100% comprehensive – for German vehicles, particularly, the records no longer exist which

would unravel the multiplicity of chassis and body types which were constructed. And even though many interesting types were under development towards the end of the conflict, purely-experimental vehicles have been purposely excluded, as have all armoured fighting vehicles.

Many different sources have been consulted in an attempt to build-up an accurate picture of this fascinating period and common sense has been used to attempt to resolve conflicts in different sources of information. Sadly, any errors which have been introduced are almost certainly due to my own lapse of concentration.

1 | Utility Vehicles

Until the advent of the mighty Jeep, the multi-purpose military utility vehicle was, perhaps, best seen as the 1940s equivalent of today's estate car or light pick-up truck, serving as both load carrier and passenger car, and almost invariably featuring rear-wheel drive.

Such vehicles tended to be car-derived… often consisting of little more than the front end of a standard 10 or 12hp light car attached to a steel pick-up body, perhaps with oversized wheels and heavy-duty suspension. The lack of all-wheel drive necessarily limited their performance off the road, and tended to mean that they were reserved for use behind the front line.

The development of the US Army's Jeep in 1940/41 changed the rules completely. With its rugged minimal construction, powerful engine and selectable four-wheel drive, the Jeep set the standard for all subsequent military utility vehicles, making machines such as the British 'Tillies' look very old fashioned indeed.

More than just a personnel carrier or light truck, the Jeep proved itself to be enormously versatile and, alongside its basic roles, ended up serving as a field ambulance, anti-tank and machine-gun mount, light recovery vehicle, artillery tractor and communications vehicle.

After the war, manufacturers all over the world started to produce Jeep-like vehicles for civilian and military use, and the genealogy of the Jeep can be traced through post-war vehicles such as the American M151, the Austin Champ, Land Rover, Toyota Land Cruiser, and Mercedes *Geländewagen*… and even the current massive US Army HMMWV (high-mobility multi-purpose wheeled vehicle).

Even today, more than 60 years since the designer Karl Probst put pen to paper, the spirit of the Jeep lives on through a myriad of modern sport utility vehicles.

Australia

Although rather oddly described as 'vans', the 1-ton chassis supplied by Chevrolet, Ford, International and Plymouth were typical Australian 'utes'. The Chevrolet consisted of a locally-built Holden steel body on an imported 1941 Chevrolet truck chassis, and the Ford,

Above: Hardly utilitarian and almost certainly unlikely to venture far from paved surfaces, the Mercedes-Benz G4 6x4 heavy motorcar was much favoured by Hitler's senior staff. Just 57 examples were produced between 1933 and 1934. Self-locking differentials in the rear axles provided some measure of off-road performance. (UB)

Left: At the other end of the scale was the ubiquitous American 4x4 Jeep. Almost 640,000 examples of the standardised MB/GPW were produced by Ford and Willys between 1941 and 1945 and the vehicle was used by all ranks. (ST)

Above: Whilst the extreme upper echelons of the Nazi party used the G4 Mercedes, German high commanders in the field were forced to make do with the likes of this essentially-civilian Auto-Union Horch 40 *Kommandeurwagen*. (UB)

International and Plymouth trucks were militarised versions of commercial vehicles.

The Chevrolet C15 and Ford F15A 'staff utility' vehicles consisted of an Australian-built body on a 1942 Canadian Military Pattern (CMP) 15cwt chassis, rather in the style of the British Humber heavy utility.

Canada

Early Canadian utility vehicles consisted of a couple of militarised Ford station wagons and a so-called 'heavy utility' constructed by the British coach-building companies Mulliner and Steward & Arden on a Ford CMP chassis.

Rather more 'military' in style was the purpose-made Chevrolet C8A six-seater heavy utility constructed by GM Ottawa on the standard CMP 4x4 chassis, powered by the 3548cc Chevrolet 'stove bolt six' engine. Aside from the personnel role, the vehicle was also used for wireless, computor (*sic*), machinery and ambulance applications. Some 13,000 examples were constructed in all.

Germany

The German Army employed a huge selection of two-, four- and even six-wheel drive passenger cars, many of which were constructed on what was effectively a standardised light truck chassis

and could be considered to be closer to the 5cwt and 8cwt trucks used by the Allies.

The VW Type 82 *Kübelwagen* was the closest thing to a utility vehicle, or to the US Army's Jeep, that the *Wehrmacht* possessed. With its flat-panelled open bodywork, it was derived from the Porsche-designed Beetle, sharing the car's unburstable air-cooled flat-four engine - initially 985cc but upgraded to 1131cc in 1943. It also used the same four-speed gearbox and torsion-bar suspension. Ground clearance was increased compared to the car by the use of drop-down reduction gears at the rear hubs. It lacked four-wheel drive but there was a limited-slip differential, and its light weight and unstressed air-cooled engine gave it a go-anywhere capability that allowed it to operate in the icy wastes of the Russian winter or the heat of the North African desert. It was certainly the equal of, and sometimes exceeded, the performance of the American icon.

Around 52,000 were produced between 1940 and 1945.

Aside from the *Kübelwagen* and the other military variants of the little VW, the German Army employed an enormous variety of passenger cars, adapted for a range of military roles for which Britain, Canada or the USA would have employed light trucks and utilities. Early vehicles were largely of civilian pattern with military bodywork, but after about 1937, standardised motor car chassis were produced

Above and left:
Although the VW Type 82 *Kübelwagen* offered a degree of off-road performance, the Wehrmacht had no equivalent of the all-wheel drive Jeep. The vehicle first appeared in 1939 and about 52,000 had been produced by the time production ended in 1945. It shared engine and suspension components with the Beetle car but featured step-down gearcases in the rear drive-line. *(UB)*

and were described either as 'light' (leicht), with engines up to 1500cc, 'medium' (mittler), 1500-3000cc, and 'heavy' (schwerer), over 3000cc. Most of the major German motor manufacturers were involved, including Horch, Stoewer, Mercedes-Benz, and Opel; there was some commonality of chassis and engine designs but it was rather half-hearted and could hardly be described as standardisation.

The Austrian Steyr-Puch company was also commissioned to build field cars for German officers, as were Tatra and Skoda in Czechoslovakia, both of these used air-cooled engines, as did Phänomen. Most of the standardised vehicles, with the exception of the 6x4 types intended for the highest-ranking officers, were fitted with purpose-designed military bodywork and often with four-wheel drive.

As with all German standard military vehicles, the role of the vehicle was indicated by a *Kraftfahrzeug* (Kfz) number; for example, numbers Kfz1-10 were assigned to light cars, Kfz.11-20 indicated medium cars, and Kfz21-30 were reserved for heavy cars, broadly as follows:

Above: The *Kübelwagen's* air-cooled engine made it eminently suitable for use wherever the Wehrmacht chose to prosecute the war... it was equally at home in the cold of the Russian winter as it was in the North African deserts. *(ST)*

Right: In the early 1930s the *Wehrmacht* specified large numbers of personnel carriers constructed on light, medium and heavy motorcar chassis. Most were available with 4x2 and 4x4 drive-lines and many also featured four-wheel steering. This is Stoewer 40 Kfz.3 light car which featured all-round independent suspension. *(PR)*

Kfz1	Light car, cross-country		Kfz11	Medium car, cross-country
Kfz1/20	Light car, cross-country, amphibious		Kfz12	Medium car, cross-country; command vehicle; tractor for anti-tank gun
Kfz2	Intelligence vehicle; radio vehicle			
Kfz2/40	Small repair vehicle		Kfz13	Medium car, machine-gun
Kfz3	Light survey section vehicle		Kfz14	Medium car, radio
Kfz4	Light car, anti-aircraft unit		Kfz15	Medium car, radio; intelligence

Kfz16	Medium car, flash and sound-ranging	Kfz18	Medium car, emergency repair
Kfz16/1	Medium car, alert	Kfz19	Medium car, telephone installation
Kfz17	Medium car, radio; cable-measuring; telephone installation	Kfz21	Heavy car, cross-country
		Kfz23	Heavy car, telephone installation
Kfz17/1	Medium car, radio	Kfz24	Heavy car, maintenance

The use of these codes was abandoned in 1943.

Above: Auto-Union Horch 40 medium staff car with accommodation for five men. Powered by a V8 petrol engine, this type was favoured by Rommel. *(ST)*

Left: Another Horch, this time the Kfz.21 heavy command car, this example was actually the personal property of Rommel and was fully restored in Germany during 2006, following its re-appearance in South Africa, and was reunited with its former driver. *(ST)*

Right: The British Army used large numbers of these 10-12hp light utilities - dubbed 'tillies - for general purpose light duties. Examples were built by Austin, Morris, Standard and, as seen here, Hillman. All were based on contemporary passenger cars. *(PW)*

Right: Humber 8cwt 4x2 truck. Slightly larger than a 'Tilly', the Humber was derived from the company's Super Snipe saloon. *(TM)*

Right: Known colloquially as 'The Box', the 4x4 Humber FWD heavy utility was used as officer transport in the field. The same chassis, with its independent front suspension, was also used for the Humber armoured light reconnaissance vehicle. *(PW)*

Right: The Jeep was standardised in 1940, with almost identical vehicles built by Ford and Willys. Early examples lacked the rear-mounted jerrycan and were stamped with the maker's name on the rear panel. These three vehicles are about to be loaded into a transport aircraft. *(RAFM)*

Below: In the hands of the Long Range Desert Group (LRDG) and the SAS, bristling with weapons and hung about with fuel, food and equipment, the Jeep set the style for what has become known as the desert patrol vehicle. Able to operate for days behind enemy lines, troops in these well-equipped vehicles were able to roam at will, destroying fuel and ammunition dumps before melting back into the desert. *(PW)*

Great Britain

The British light utility vehicle, affectionately known as the 'Tilly' was a small pick-up truck derived from a standard civilian saloon car. It was one of those typical British wartime improvisations which didn't quite succeed, even on its own terms, and yet somehow managed to survive against the odds. Four manufacturers were involved, and despite the vehicle being rated for a 10cwt load, all were grossly underpowered and, lacking four-wheel drive, offered very limited cross-country performance.

The Austin was the most prolific of the four types available, basing its model on the very conventional leaf-sprung chassis and steel cab of the pre-war side-valve engined 10hp car. Large numbers were also built by Morris and Hillman, with both manufacturers also using their 10hp chassis; Hillman also produced a van version. The smallest producer was the Standard Motor Company, who employed their 12hp vehicle as the basis.

'Tillies' were used by British and British Commonwealth troops and, despite the delivery of thousands of Jeeps into British Army service,

Above: There had been an earlier version based on the 8hp General Post Office (GPO) van, but the standard Morris 'Tilly' was based on the company's 10hp Series M motorcar. *(ST)*

Right: With its independent front suspension and all-wheel drive, the Humber FWD chassis as used for 'The Box' also provided the basis for a useful 8cwt personnel/cargo vehicle. *(ST)*

Above: Ford WOA2 heavy utility. Although it lacked front-wheel drive, the powerful V8 engine and roomy, four-door steel body made the Ford a useful vehicle which remained in production beyond the end of the war. *(ST)*

Left: With a decidedly pre-war timber-framed body, the Humber 'Box' seems to belong to a different era altogether. *(ST)*

Right: A Bianchi S4 four-seater light car dating from 1938. 100 of which were supplied to the Italian War Ministry. The Italian leader Benito Mussolini is on a tour of defences, 29 June 1940. *(UB)*

Above: Japanese Kurogane 4x4 scout car. Designed by Rikuo in 1935, the diminutive Type 95 field car must have been one of the smallest all-wheel drive vehicles produced during the World War Two. There was also a pick-up variant. *(PW)*

the little 'Tilly' served throughout the war and well into the 1950s, typically as a behind-the-lines personnel transport or general load carrier.

Falling somewhere between being a small truck and an estate car, the so-called 'heavy utility' was another matter, with curiously dissimilar vehicles from Ford and Humber being assigned the same description. Chiefly used as staff cars, Humber's contribution was the rear-wheel drive Snipe estate car, which was also procured in saloon and tourer form, and the all-wheel drive FWD, better known as the 'Box', which shared its chassis, six-cylinder side-valve engine and running gear with Humber's light reconnaissance vehicle. Ford constructed the WOA2 estate car with a big all-steel estate car body and side-valve V8 engine derived from the pre-war 22HP car range; like the Snipe, it lacked all-wheel drive.

Italy

Rather in the mould of the British Army's 'Tillies', the Fiat 508C Mil was a light truck with wooden half-doors and an open-topped wooden cargo bed; a staff car version was also produced and a long-wheelbase version (508 LRM) was used to mount dual 20mm anti-aircraft guns. It was derived from the pre-war Fiat Balilla 1100 car and was produced from 1939, replacing an earlier vehicle of the same designation.

There was independent front suspension, and the vehicle was powered by a four-cylinder engine. Load capacity was 772lb (350kg).

Conceived as a scout car and light truck, the Jeep was pressed into service in a variety of roles, there were even flying conversions. Here we see an armoured patrol vehicle (below), armed with a .30 calibre Browning machine gun, together with what must have been an early exponent of the 'shoot and scoot' philosophy, armed with both .50 and .30 calibre Browning. *(JSS)*

Japan

The only Japanese utility vehicle was the pick-up variant of the Rikuo-designed Kurogane Type 95 which went into production in 1936. Very much in the mould of the British 'Tilly', the Kurogane had an enclosed steel cab and a small canvas-covered pick-up body. Powered by an air-cooled V-twin engine of 1,399cc, suspension was independent at the front by means of coil springs, with a leaf-sprung live axle at the rear. A total of 4,775 were produced, including the passenger car variant.

Soviet Union

The Soviet Union received some 20,000 American Jeeps as part of the Lend-Lease arrangements, but also developed their own vehicle along similar lines. Produced by the Gorkiy Automobile Plant, the first incarnation was the prototype GAZ-64 which appeared in 1941. By late 1942, at which time only 686 had been built, the GAZ-64 was replaced by the improved GAZ-67 and GAZ-67B, the latter coming in 1943, and featured a widened wheel track and an uprated engine.

Extraordinarily ungainly in appearance, and crude in construction, the GAZ-64/67 was powered by a four-cylinder engine of 3,285cc based on pre-war technology which had been bought from the Ford Motor Company of the USA. The engine was coupled to a four-speed gearbox and two-speed transfer case, and the front axle could be disengaged when not required. Rigid, live axles were suspended on leaf springs, with twinned

Above: Long Range Desert Group (LRDG) Jeep armed with three Vickers K machine guns, and a .50 calibre Browning. The road tyres were favoured fitment for the front wheels when operating in desert conditions. The enthusiast owner has recreated and exact replica of a LRDG jeep. (ST)

Right: All of the Allies, and all arms of service used the Jeep... indeed, it is difficult to imagine a successful outcome to the war without the ubiquitous 1/4-ton 4x4 produced by Ford and Willys. (ST)

Above: Replica of the Wasp flame-thrower equipped Jeep used by Popski's Private Army. Popski was another of those maverick characters who thrived during the World War Two, harassing the enemy behind the lines. The flame thrower equipment was taken from a Universal Carrier, and by all accounts took the hair and eyebrows off the operator the first time it was used. (PR)

Left: The Red Army received thousands of Jeeps under the Lend-Lease arrangements but also built their own 4x4 scout car, the GAZ-67. Using technology licensed from Ford, the GAZ-67B was the most numerous variant, with nearly 63,000 built between 1942 and 1953. (ST)

quarter-elliptic springs at the front. The brakes were mechanically operated.

The slab-sided, angular bodywork was cut away at the sides in the style of the US-built Jeep and the windscreen could be folded down onto the bonnet.

The GAZ-67 remained in production until 1953 by which time almost 63,000 had been produced.

United States of America

Until the development of the Jeep in 1940, US Army vehicles used for the utility role consisted of a miscellany of essentially civilian-type station wagons, vans/carryalls and light pick-up trucks, typically supplied by Ford, Chevrolet, and Dodge (see page 26).

The Jeep was the first US Army vehicle to actually be described as a 'utility', although it was later re-designated simply as a 'truck'. Karl E. Probst is generally considered to be the 'father' of the Jeep, but the vehicle was actually a joint effort. Outline designs and specifications were prepared by US Quartermaster Corps (QMC) and these were developed into a prototype by Probst, freelancing for American

Bantam. Having seen Bantam's design, Willys-Overland and Ford Motor Company engineers subsequently produced their own versions.

The three prototypes were produced and tested in late 1940 and, unable to decide between them, the QMC ordered 1,500 of each design… at this stage known as the Bantam 40-BRC, Willys MA, and Ford GP. The 1/4-ton load rating allowed the little vehicle to carry four personnel or a quantity of supplies, although the lack of a hinged tailgate hindered loading.

By 1941 the design was standardised as the Willys MB and the Ford GPW. The standardised Jeep was effectively Ford's version of the Bantam design, powered by the 2,199cc Willys Go-Devil engine; all parts were interchangeable between the two vehicles, which could only be told apart by relatively minor details. Despite having probably made the greatest contribution to the development of what was a new type of military vehicle, Bantam received no further contracts.

Relatively light weight, combined with a three-speed gearbox and selectable all-wheel drive via a two-speed transfer case, gave excellent off-road performance, even if the rather primitive leaf-spring suspension and live axles resulted in a harsh ride. The open bodywork gave minimal weather protection but canvas side-screens could be fitted to provide a complete enclosure; the windscreen could be folded down onto the flat bonnet to reduce the overall profile.

Some 650,000 were constructed by the time production ended in 1945, with Willys producing the majority. Jeeps were used by the US Army and supplied to all of the Allies under the Lend-lease arrangements.

The Jeep quickly replaced the motorcycle, proving itself indispensable for a variety of tasks ranging from simple passenger-carrying duties, through reconnaissance missions, and load carrying, even serving as a gun platform and artillery tractor. There were even amphibious (see page 150) and armoured versions, and a couple of brave attempts to make it fly… a number were even converted for use as railway locomotives!

Dating from 1943, the Waukesha-powered Crosley CT-3 Pup was the only possible competitor to the Jeep to be procured in any number, with some 36 examples purchased and despatched overseas for (unsuccessful) trials.

2 | Light Trucks up to 2 tons

In mechanised warfare trucks provide essential logistical support, carrying men, ammunition, weapons, food, clothing, fuel and every type of ordnance supplies, often over unmade roads and shattered ground. Despite this all-wheel drive trucks were not universal during the war, and most participants in the conflict continued to procure both road-going and cross-country vehicles, the former, of course, being cheaper and easier to maintain.

Whilst the lack of all-wheel-drive vehicles may have occasionally caused difficulties, far more serious were the problems faced by Great Britain and Germany as a result of having too many makes and types of vehicle in service. Clearly the trucks required dedicated logistical support, and it does not require much imagination to see the advantages of buying a small number of standardised models. Not only does this mean that drivers and mechanics require less training, but it also reduces the need for parts stockholding which, in turn, reduces the requirement for transportation, freeing up space for more important supplies like guns and ammunition!

The German Army had attempted to avoid this problem by devising a complex system of classification by standardisation of both chassis and body type for trucks and cars, which allowed vehicles of the same type to be constructed by a number of manufacturers. However, the cost of the specialised military vehicles combined with the 'needs must' approach of the later years of the

war meant that the so-called standardisation all became rather academic, and vehicles were pressed into service which would never have formed part of the original plan.

There is a tendency to think that US-built trucks were heavily standardised because there were so many examples of standard types such as the $^{3}/_{4}$ ton Dodge series and the $2^{1}/_{2}$ ton GMC but, in truth, the US Army employed almost as many different types of truck as did the Germans and the British. However, many of the US designs remained in production for the entire duration of the war virtually without modification.

Of the major participants in World War Two, it was Canada that was most successful at standardisation, developing a relatively small range of vehicles which could be built by more than one manufacturer.

Note: The definition of 'light trucks' has been borrowed from *Wehrmacht* practice where any truck below 2 tons was considered as 'light'. Whilst this does not exactly accord with British

Above: Typical of impressed vehicles used by the *Wehrmacht* is this Renault 1.5-tonne model AGC. Produced between 1936 and 1940, the AGC was one of a series of similar trucks produced by the French company, in this instance powered by a 2,383cc engine. The radiator cover suggests the Eastern Front. *(UB)*

Left: The British Fordson WOT2 was a 15cwt 4x2 chassis which was generally bodied as an open cargo vehicle, as here, but could also be fitted with a van body. *(ST)*

Right: A Praga RV 6x4 *Funkwagen* (radio truck). These trucks were built between 1936 and 1939 for export and for the Czechoslovak Army. Many were commandeered by the Germans when the country surrendered on 14 March 1939. *(UB)*

Below: The *Wehrmacht* used numbers of the 2-ton RV Praga 6x4 vehicles fitted with a variety of different bodies. *(PW)*

or US thinking of the period it avoids the anomaly of having 'light' trucks from one nation compared to 'medium' trucks of another.

Australia

Australia tended to use trucks of both British and US manufacture, the latter supplied under Lend-Lease. Local-built vehicles were a rarity.

Most notable of the latter is the locally-assembled and bodied Canadian Military Pattern (CMP) 15cwt Chevrolet C15A. The chassis and other components were imported from Canada, with cabs and bodies constructed by GM Holden, these included office, cargo, wireless and fire tender versions.

Canada

Canadian Military Pattern (CMP) vehicles were probably the most successful standardised trucks of World War Two, combining British War Office-pattern cabs and bodies with US automotive

engineering. Both Ford and Chevrolet (GM) produced trucks ranging from 8cwt 4x2 to 3 ton 6x6 to virtually identical designs, and between them the two companies produced 815,000 military vehicles during the war.

The bottom end of the 'light' category includes the 8cwt Chevrolet C8 and Ford F8 4x2 trucks which were produced only as general service (GS) cargo or wireless vehicles. The heavier C15 and F15 variants were rated at 15cwt and were produced in both 4x2 and 4x4 form; aside from the 'heavy utility' variant which has already been covered, typical roles included GS cargo, battery charging, wireless, radio location, machinery and water tanker. The 30cwt C30/F30 chassis was produced only in 4x4 form and was bodied as a GS cargo or communications vehicle, ambulance and artillery tractor.

The Chevrolet MCP 1533X2 was a modified civilian 30cwt truck much favoured by the British Long Range Desert Group (LRDG).

The 8cwt Dodge T212 resembled the early ¹/₂ ton US Army pick-ups produced by this

Above: A captured British Morris-Commercial CS8 15cwt cargo/infantry truck in use by the *Fallschirmjäger* in Heraklion, Crete, 29 May 1941. Many of these trucks were abandoned in France after the evacuation of the British Expeditionary Force in 1940. *(UB)*

Above: Unable to produce sufficient trucks at home, the *Wehrmacht* was not averse to using captured vehicles, particularly in France. Whilst not a type that served with the French Army, nor representative of the French trucks supplied to the *Wehrmacht*, this restored Renault ADK, derived from the contemporary *Primaquatre*. *(PR)*

Right: 1^1/$_2$-ton Steyr 1500A 4x4 light truck fitted with the *Einheits* cab. Constructed from timber framing and pressed fibreboard it was used to replace the standard steel item. *(ST)*

Left: Italian OM Autocarretta. Dating from 1932, this was an unusual light truck/artillery tractor which featured four-wheel steering and four-wheel drive, and which for much of its life continued to run on solid tyres. *(AN)*

Left: Italian SPA CL39 1-ton 4x4 truck. This is the so-called 'colonial' version and, although it dates from 1940, a contemporary variant was still running on solid tyres. *(AN)*

Left: A 1941 $\frac{1}{2}$-ton Dodge WC 4x4 pick-up truck. From 1941 the WC was succeded by the $\frac{3}{4}$-ton T214 which was built in very large numbers up to the end of the war. *(PR)*

Right: The Adler HK300/A1 was prototyped in 1938/39 as a possible contender for the light semi-track role. *(JSS)*

Right: The second Adler light semi-track prototype was the HK300/A2 which appeared in 1939. *(JSS)*

Right: The Demag D7 (qv) was the successful contender for the light semi-track role. Its predecessor, the D6 of 1937/38, seen here, was the last development vehicle in the series before production was started. *(JSS)*

company but was fitted with a British War Office-type steel body. Dodge (Canada) also produced a version of the ¾ ton WC52 winch-equipped weapons carrier, with minor body modifications and a larger capacity six-cylinder petrol engine.

Germany

In re-arming in the 1930s, Germany had sponsored the design and manufacture of a range of beautifully-engineered military vehicles but there was insufficient production capacity available and these were soon joined by a miscellany of impressed, confiscated and commercial types. The result was that there were too many vehicle types in service, with standardisation restricted to weight classes and use. The Schell Programme of 1938 was an attempt to bring some order to this chaos by specifying a restricted range of both civilian and military pattern vehicles which could be produced more quickly and at lower cost, often by more than one company; many of the more sophisticated vehicle types were abandoned as being unreliable and too costly. Trucks were produced in the light (leicht), medium (mittler) and heavy (schwerer) classes.

As the war progressed, Germany became desperately short of transport. Confiscated vehicles from the armies of occupied nations were pressed into service, often alongside civilian type vehicles purchased (or confiscated) from manufacturers in those countries; even captured army vehicles were used.

The multiplicity of types in service makes it difficult to single out any one type as being representative, but the standardised all-wheel-drive light cargo vehicle – *leichtergeländegänig-Einheitslastkraftwage*n, (leglELkw) was still a relatively sophisticated vehicle, with coil-sprung independent suspension, diesel engine and six-wheel drive. Examples were produced by Borgward, Büssing-NAG, FAUN, Henschel, Magirus and MAN.

Typical of the products of the mid-1930s was the Krupp L2H43, a 6x4 light truck powered by a 3,000cc four-cylinder air-cooled engine driving through a four-speed gearbox and two-speed transfer case. The vehicle featured independent

Above: On the far left, a 6x4 Magirus M206 light truck (1934-37) is flanked by a pair of Austro-Daimler AGR 6x4 3-tonners. (UB)

Below: Czech-built Praga RVR 6x4 light truck in use with the *Wehrmacht* as a *Funkwagen* (radio vehicle). A command car version was built on the same chassis. (JSS)

Right: 8cwt Canadian Military Pattern (CMP) 4x2 wireless or personnel truck. The vehicle was constructed by both Ford (as the F8) or Chevrolet (C8) to an almost identical pattern, each company using their own engine. *(PR)*

Right: A late model Ford WOT2E with steel doors and semi-enclosed cab. Around 60,000 of these V8-powered 15cwt trucks were supplied between 1939 and 1945. *(ST)*

Right: Very rare amongst the British 15cwt trucks is the Guy Ant, produced in both 4x2 (shown) and 4x4 form between 1938 and 1944. *(ST)*

Left: Humber FWD 8cwt cargo/personnel truck; the same chassis was also used as the basis for an ambulance, staff car, and wireless vehicle. *(ST)*

Left: Early Bedford MWD 4x2 15cwt cargo vehicle. Some 66,000 of these 15cwt trucks were built between 1939 and 1945. *(ST)*

Left: A very capable vehicle, the Dodge WC51/WC52 ¾-ton 4x4 weapons carrier was used by all of the Allies and by all arms of service. This example is in the markings of the US Navy. *(ST)*

Above: Early Ford WOT2C infantry truck. Note the aero screens and lack of doors, typical of pre-war British military vehicles. *(IWM)*

rear suspension by coil springs and had self-locking differentials. Initially entering production in 1933, it was replaced by the similar L2H143 in 1937 with production continuing until 1942. Produced as a gun tractor, staff car, personnel carrier, and radio vehicle, the vehicle was also fitted with a number of armoured body types.

As with all purpose-designed German military vehicles, the role of the vehicle was indicated by a *SonderKraftfahrzeug* (SdKfz) number. Bodies typically installed on the 'light' chassis were as follows:

SdKfz61	Telephone generator; teletype; radio; radio beacon; cable survey; maintenance
SdKfz62	Printing press; flash detector; sound detector; sound plotting; meteorology
SdKfz63	Flash detector
SdKfz64	Range finder; measurement range
SdKfz68	Radio antenna
SdKfz69	Maintenance; artillery limber
SdKfz70	Personnel carrier; amplifier van
SdKfz76	Observation balloon cable
SdKfz77	Telephone cable
SdKfz79	Repair workshop
SdKfz81	Anti-aircraft unit

The use of these codes was abandoned in 1943.

Germany also favoured half-track vehicles as both personnel carriers and gun tractors. Most numerous of these was the SdKfz10, a standardised Maybach-engined light half-track designed by Demag as the D7. The vehicle was also produced by Adler, Büssing-NAG, Maschinen Werke Cottbus (MWC) and Saurer.

Lower-cost, road-going trucks of the Schell Programme were supplied by Borgward, Opel, Mercedes-Benz and the Austrian company Steyr. After the occupation of France in 1940 trucks were also procured from both Renault and Citroën.

Great Britain

Like the US, the British had attempted to standardise on load classes – using categories of 8cwt, 15cwt, 30cwt, 3 tons, 6 tons and 10 tons – but had generally been unable to standardise on design, which meant that widely dissimilar

Left: Morris-Commercial CS8 15cwt 4x2 truck. This chassis went into production in 1934, initially with an open cab and roll-up canvas doors. It was replaced by the C8 in 1944. *(PW)*

vehicles in the same load class were being supplied by a number of manufacturers.

A reluctance to spend money on defence during the 1930s meant that Britain entered World War Two with a large number of ageing trucks; the 6x4 Morris-Commercial CD, for example, dated from 1933. To make matters worse, so many vehicles were left behind during the retreat of the British Expeditionary Force from Northern France in 1940 (more than 5,000 of the 30cwt-class vehicles alone were abandoned) that the War Department could scarcely afford to turn down anything which the domestic motor industry could produce. It was not until around 1941 – and thanks to some assistance from the US government – that British problems with transport started to improve.

The 8cwt class was never much more than a pick-up truck, being too small to be of any real use and it was soon abandoned.

Vehicles worthy of mention in the light class include the Bedford MW which, if not the first, was certainly the most successful and numerous of the many 15cwt vehicles which entered production in the mid-1930s; aside from the cargo body, it was

also fitted as a water tanker, anti-aircraft gun mount, gun portee and machinery truck. Bedford also contributed the 30cwt OX, which was eventually superseded by the 3 ton OY. The 15cwt Morris-Commercial CS and C4 models were also constructed in large numbers up to 1944, although the design dated back to 1934; wireless and GS variants were the most numerous. A 4x4 version was also built. Ford built approximately 60,000 examples of the similar WOT2 truck.

Above: Bedford OXD, a 4x2 30cwt cargo truck. The same chassis was also used as the basis of the OXC tractor for semi-trailer. *(PW)*

Right: Filling the fuel tanks of a Bedford MWD 4x2 15cwt cargo truck using a hand-operated pump. *(PW)*

Below: With all-steel construction, powerful six-cylinder engine, and all-wheel drive, the low-profile $^3/_4$-ton Dodge WC51 and WC52 (the latter winch equipped as shown) was far superior to the essentially pre-war design of equivalent British trucks. *(PW)*

British vehicles of this period were generally of very straightforward design, with simple live axles and leaf-spring suspension. Side-valve petrol engines were usually fitted for simplicity and reliability.

Large numbers of US and Canadian-built vehicles were also used by the British Army.

India

Light truck chassis produced by both Chevrolet and Ford were assembled in India from Completely-Knocked-Down (CKD) kits, and were fitted with locally-built bodies.

Large numbers of British and US-built vehicles were also used by the Indian Army.

Italy

Italian Army trucks were classed as light (*leggero*), medium (*medio*) and heavy (*pesante*), with standardised designs produced in the medium and heavy classes. Specialised military designs in the light class were produced by OM and the Fiat-controlled SPA.

The smallest Italian trucks were based on the Fiat 508C 'Mil' which was derived from the 1937 Balilla 1100 car chassis. The vehicle was rated at 772lb (350kg) capacity and featured independent front suspension and a 1,089cc overhead-valve petrol engine. The larger Fiat 508L was rated at 1,323lb (600kg) and the 618 at 2,866lb (1,300kg) payload.

The curious-looking SPA CL39 was produced by the Soc Ligure Piemontese Automobili and first appeared in 1937, remaining in production until 1948. The forward-control CL39 and the similar CLF39 infantry truck were powered by a 1,628cc four-cylinder petrol engine; the CLF39 was equipped with pneumatic tyres, the CL39 cargo variant had solid tyres. The AL37 'Sahara' and TL37 were light trucks (*autocarrero leggero or autocarretta*) of very short-wheelbase 4x4 design, featuring large 24in (61cm) wheels and four-wheel steering, the TL37 being a gun tractor. SPA also produced the AS37, a 1-ton light truck of more conventional appearance.

Most interesting of the Italian trucks is the rather old-fashioned looking OM Autocarretta 32, a 4x4 general-purpose forward-control truck which had been first produced by Ansaldo but which was later manufactured by Officine Meccaniche (OM), a Fiat subsidiary. Twin transverse leaf springs were used to provide independent suspension at front and rear, with lockable differentials. The truck was powered by a four-cylinder air-cooled diesel engine, driving through a

Right: Ford WOT3D, a 30cwt 4x2 chassis equipped with an RAF workshop body. Some 18,000 of these trucks were produced with a variety of bodies. *(RAFM)*

centrally-mounted gearbox and auxiliary gear; steering was provided on all four wheels. The original Tipo 32 had solid tyres but this was superseded by the Tipo 36M in 1936 and the Tipo 37 a year later; like the SPA products, both had an extremely short, 79in (2.01m), wheelbase.

When the Italian fascist government fell in 1943, the occupying German forces tried, with very little success, to get Fiat to produce trucks for the German Army.

Japan

Aside from the Kurogane and other motor-tricycles, production of which exceeded that of trucks during the inter-war period, Japanese

Right: 15cwt 4x2 Commer Q2 chassis equipped with a special Mulliners-built van body for RAF use. Production started in July 1940. *(RAFM)*

Left: Humber FWD 8cwt 4x4 ambulance which has been fitted with a sound-recording body for the BBC. *(TM)*

trucks in the light class were produced by Isuzu, Nissan and Toyota, with little development taking place during the years of the conflict. A Government subsidy scheme encouraged civilian customers to purchase trucks, which could subsequently be impressed into military service, a scheme which had been tried in Europe before World War One.

Isuzu's contribution was the Type 94, the design of which was heavily influenced by a number of imported Scammell, Tatra and Thornycroft trucks. The vehicle was a conventional 6x4 truck of typical mid-1930s design and powered by a 4,390cc, water-cooled petrol engine; Type 94B was diesel engined. A 4x2 variant was also produced. The YOK1 model was a

Left: Morris-Commercial PU8/4 8cwt 4x4 wireless truck. Approximately 1,200 such vehicles produced in 1942, others were equipped with a personnel/cargo body. *(TM)*

Right: The 8cwt Morris-Commercial PU was introduced in 1936. It was the rear-wheel drive variant of the PU8/4 chassis and was fitted with a standardised cargo body which could be removed and used as a shelter, being supported on the folding legs. *(TM)*

Right: Commer Q15 4x2 15cwt cargo truck. A lightly-militarised Commer Superpoise civilian type. The vehicle was supplied to the RAF from late 1940. *(PW)*

2 ton 4x4 design and the ROK1 was the 6x6 variant. Both vehicles were introduced in 1942, but were only produced in limited numbers.

The Nissan 80 and 180 were $1^{1}/_{2}$ ton 4x2 trucks of conventional layout, powered by a 3,670cc six-cylinder side-valve water-cooled petrol engine based on that used by the Graham Paige Motor Company. The Type 80 was of semi-forward control layout and the Type 180, although mechanically similar, was a conventional bonnetted truck.

The Toyota AK was a $^{1}/_{2}$ ton 4x2 truck based on the AA motorcar. The GB was a six-cylinder $1^{1}/_{2}$ ton 4x2 based on a 1936 Chevrolet design;

some 20,000 of these were produced between 1938 and 1942 for both military and civilian use.

Soviet Union

The Soviet Union produced very few light trucks, instead relying on enormous numbers of Lend-Lease vehicles from the US, including Dodge weapons carriers and Chevrolet and Dodge $1^{1}/_{2}$ ton trucks. By the end of the war the Soviet Union had received more than 400,000 trucks and other vehicles from the US.

Several Soviet trucks were produced in the medium and heavy classes, but the Red Army

Above: GAZ-AAA 1¹/₂-ton 6x4 truck. A development of the GAZ-AA truck, some 37,500 examples were built between 1934 and 1943 in a wide range of variants. *(AN)*

Left: Soviet GAZ-MM-V 1¹/₂-ton 4x2 cargo truck. Produced between 1941 and 1945, this was a simplified version of the civilian GAZ AA truck. *(AN)*

fielded just two basic types of light truck of domestic origin, both of which were basically standard commercial vehicles. The GAZ-AA, and the GAZ-MM, were 1¹/₂ ton 4x2 cargo vehicles powered by the standard GAZ four-cylinder petrol engine of 3,285cc; the GAZ-AAA was an otherwise similar 6x4 design. Over 1,000,000 examples were produced during the almost 20 years that the vehicles were in production.

A half-track version of the GAZ-AAA was produced in 1938, using a Kégresse type bogie; this was designated GAZ-60. Similarly, the ZIS-33 was a half-track conversion of the civilian ZIS-5, although it used a very simple rear bogie which retained the standard road wheels, and the GAZ-VM *Pikap* was a half-track version of the GAZ-M1 truck.

United States of America

During World War One, and into the 1920s, the US Army had attempted to develop a range of standardised military vehicles but was forced to virtually abandon the initiative in the face of budgetary constraints. By 1935 the US Quartermaster Corps' (QMC) policy of buying purely commercial vehicles led to there being

Right: Japanese forces enter Peking, China, 31 July 1937. The light tank is at the head of a column of Isuzu Type 94 trucks. *(UB)*

Left and far left:
The 1 $\frac{1}{2}$-ton Isuzu Type 94 appeared in 1934 and was the Japan's Imperial Army standard cross-country truck. Based on typical European practice of the early 1930s, it feautured a 6x4 drive-line, and was produced in a variety of configurations. The Type 94A was powered by a petrol engine, the 94B used a diesel power unit. *(PW)*

Above: The ³/₄-ton Dodge WC series was constructed for a number of different roles. This is the WC53 Carryall of which some 8,400 examples were built between 1942 and 1943. *(ST)*

Right: The Ford GTB was a low-profile 1¹/₂-ton 4x4 truck built for the US Army and Navy between 1942 and 1944. Most were bodied as cargo vehicles (designated GTBA), but some 4,700 were equipped as bomb service vehicles as below (GTBC). *(ST)*

Above: The largest of the Dodge WC series was the 1¹/₂-tonne WC62/63 6x6 weapons/personnel carrier, the latter being equipped with a front-mounted winch. More than 43,000 were built from late 1942 on. *(ST)*

Left: A Ford 2G8T 1¹/₂-ton 4x2 stake truck. Although it was essentially a civilian vehicle, the US Army procured large numbers during the early years of the war. Many were converted to 4x4 configuration by the Marmon-Herrington company. *(PW)*

more than 350 different types in service, requiring a stockholding of nearly 1,000,000 different spare parts!

By 1939 it was clear that this situation could not continue, and the QMC proposed that the purchase of each vehicle type would be restricted to just two different competing commercial manufacturers. The vehicles were assigned to five load capacities... $\frac{1}{2}$ ton, $1\frac{1}{2}$ ton, $2\frac{1}{2}$ ton, 4 ton, and $7\frac{1}{2}$ ton... and were to be lightly militarised by the addition of towing eyes, and radiator and headlamp guards. But progress was slow and by June 1940 there were approved types in only three of the

classes: the $1\frac{1}{2}$-ton Dodge 4x4, the fabled $2\frac{1}{2}$-ton GMC 6x6 (see Medium trucks, page 50), and the 6 ton Mack 6x6 (see Heavy trucks, page 74). Although the success of the Jeep forced the QMC to add a $\frac{1}{4}$ ton class, and the $\frac{1}{2}$ ton class was raised to $\frac{3}{4}$ ton in view of the improvements which Dodge was able to make to the WC series, within two years the number of makes purchased was reduced from 350 to just 16.

In July 1940 the US Army had 30,000 trucks in service; within six months this number had risen to 70,000... and by December 1941 the total had reached more than 250,000.

Left: Although few have survived, Chevrolet built around 150,000 1 ½-ton G-4100 and G-7100 4x4 trucks between 1940 and 1945. Most were bodied as cargo vehicles but there were also tractors for semi-trailer use, panel vans, telephone maintenance vehicles, dump trucks, etc. Note the early Ford GP Jeeps at the bottom of the photograph. *(PW)*

US military vehicle production during the war amounted to more than 3.2 million vehicles and, with its massive industrial muscle, the USA became the arsenal of the free world producing many more transport vehicles than either Germany or Great Britain… and Roosevelt's Lend-Lease Program ensured that these trucks were available to all of the Allied armies.

The key US Army light trucks were the 1 ½ ton Chevrolet of which some 150,000 were produced and the ¾ ton Dodge WC series which was produced in a range of variants with significant commonality of parts. In total, more than 250,000 Dodge WC vehicles were produced between 1942 and 1945. Both types were of conventional design, with high-capacity six-cylinder petrol engines, heavy-duty chassis, live axles and leaf spring suspension allowing high ground clearance.

The large numbers of Fords supplied in this weight category were essentially civilian vehicles, lightly militarised.

Other types worth mentioning are the Willys MT-Tug, effectively a 6x6 version of the Jeep, of which some 15 examples were built. Also the Studebaker Weasel, a tracked carrier designed for over-snow operation, of which there was also an amphibious version (see page 50).

3 | Medium Trucks up to 3 tons

Medium trucks are considered to be those offering a payload of between 2 and 3 tons, and during the war, the $2^1/_2$ to 3-ton truck was generally the heaviest which could be mass produced. The type went on to become the backbone of both the Allied and Axis supply units, with standardised designs produced in large numbers, particularly for the US Army.

US manufacturers completed more than 750,000 on the $2^1/_2$ ton chassis from 1941, most with all-wheel drive. In Britain, over 400,000 of the 3 ton-class vehicles were put into service between 1939 and 1945. In Germany, the majority of trucks in this category were based on the Opel Blitz, basically a pre-war commercial design.

Most medium trucks were bodied as cargo vehicles, but the $2^1/_2$ to 3 ton chassis was also adapted for a wide variety of other uses, including personnel transport, tipper/dumper, office, gun tractor, workshop/machinery, signals/ communications, compressor, searchlight, canteen/ kitchen, laboratory and bridging and also for bulk transport of fuel, oil and water.

Most of the trucks in this category were of resolutely conventional design, with a forward-mounted four- or six-cylinder engine driving the wheels through a four-speed gearbox; most all-wheel-drive designs were fitted with a two-speed transfer case but locking differentials were definitely not a standard item. Whilst Britain, the

British Commonwealth countries and the US generally tended to favour petrol engines in this class, other nations were more enthusiastic about the advantages of diesel engines. Suspension was invariably by multi-leaf semi-elliptical springs and very few trucks were fitted with anything other than live beam axles. Servo-assisted brakes (usually of the vacuum type) were a common feature on the later designs.

The most significant vehicle in this category is undoubtedly the US-built GMC CCKW (C: 1941 design; C: conventional cab; K: all-wheel drive; W: tandem rear drive), a classic $2^1/_2$ ton 6x6 which, although the vehicle was developed from a civilian pre-war design, remained in production through-out the war with very little modification. It was supplied to all of the Allied armies. A rugged, well-made truck, it was supplied to all of the Allied Armies and many remained in service with US forces into the 1950s. In Europe many CCKWs serviced into the 1970s and 1980s, notably with the armies of France, Greece and Norway.

Above: The 2 1/2-ton GMC CCKW 6x6 was the mainstay of the US Army's logistical fleet, serving on all fronts throught the conflict. More than 500,000 were produced between 1941 and 1945 by Chevrolet and the Yellow Truck & Coach Manufacturing Company. There were both long- and short-wheelbase variants and the open cab was adopted from around 1942. (ST)

Left: Canadian Military Pattern (CMP) 4x4 general-service truck fitted with a British-type cargo body. Similar trucks were built by Ford (F60L) and Chevrolet (C60L). (ST)

There were experiments with halftrack cargo-carrying versions of the British-built Bedford QL and also a number of US-built chassis, including Autocar, Diamond T, Mack and White. However, only the Soviet Union and Germany put such vehicles into quantity production.

Australia

Medium trucks for the Australian Army were built mainly on imported 4x2, 4x4 and 6x6 chassis, generally of US origin and fitted with locally-built bodywork.

Australian Army tractor-trucks are interesting. A 4x2 tractor unit was designed and produced in Australia for use with a 7-ton McGrath semi-trailer for service on the east-west/north-south highways that cross that vast continent. Dating from 1942, examples were built by International Harvester (K7) and Ford (118T).

Also worthy of mention are the Australian-bodied versions of the Ford F60 and the GMC (Chevrolet) C60 Canadian Military Pattern (CMP) vehicles.

Canada

As one might expect, the larger variants of the standardised CMP vehicles made up the bulk of the Canadian Army's medium fleet, notably the 4x2 and 4x4 Ford F60 and Chevrolet C60 chassis, both of which were produced in short and long-wheelbase configurations. Some 209,000 Canadian 3-ton vehicles were constructed during the war, and these vehicles were fitted with a variety of body types including steel GS

Left: Ford of Köln produced thousands of these 3-ton V3000S 4x2 cargo vehicles between 1941 and 1945, powered by a V8 petrol engine. As the war moved on, many were fitted with the simplified front mudguards and pressed fibreboard and timber *Einheitsfahrerhaus* cab in place of the standard steel item. *(JSS)*

cargo, machinery, stores, dumper truck, office, water/fuel tanker, gun portee and recovery.

There was also a 6x6 variant on the Chevrolet C60 chassis, designated C60X and equipped as a stores truck as well as with other bodies. A similar 6x4 Ford (F60H) was built, but on this vehicle the rearmost axle was not driven. Ford also produced the 4x4 F60T for use as a tractor to tow a 6-ton semi-trailer.

The Chevrolet CC60, Dodge T110 and T130, also the Ford FC60L types were all modified civilian trucks.

Germany

In the between-the-wars period the *Wehrmacht* had tended to concentrate on the development of 6x4 and 6x6 trucks, with several manufacturers producing similar trucks to a common specification; it was felt that the use of four driving wheels at the rear obviated the need for front-wheel drive. There was no standardisation but Mercedes-Benz did produce a 6x6 which shared many components with a lighter, 4x4 and a heavier, 8x8 version of what was essentially the

same diesel-powered chassis. Diesel-powered 4x2 and 4x4 trucks were also produced by Borgward, Klockner-Deutz and Mercedes-Benz. Ford Köln (Cologne) also produced large numbers of the V3000S medium 4x2 chassis powered by a Ford V8 side-valve petrol engine.

However, the best-known of the German medium trucks is almost certainly the 3-ton Opel Blitz, a modified commercial truck powered by a 3,626cc Opel six-cylinder water-cooled petrol engine and produced in 4x2 and 4x4 configurations with a variety of different bodies; some 25,000 examples of the 4x4 were produced.

A shortage of steel towards the latter years of the war led to the development of the so-called *Einheitsfahrerhaus* (standardised cab) a cheap, graceless construction of wood and pressed fibreboard which must have offered less weather protection than the canvas-covered cabs appearing on late-war US Army trucks.

As with all purpose-designed German military vehicles, the role of the vehicle was indicated by a *SonderKraftfahrzeug* (SdKfz)

Below: A steel-cabbed Ford V3000S bogged down in the mud as a VW *Kübelwagen* struggles past. Small numbers of the V3000S were also produced with all-wheel drive. *(UB)*

number. Bodies typically installed on the 'medium' chassis were as follows:

SdKfz42	Battery charging; maintenance; radio repair
SdKfz51	Workshop
SdKfz72	Telephone exchange; teletype; radio teletype; radio; radio interception; meteorology; printing
SdKfz72/1	Teletype
SdKfz74	Anti-aircraft survey section
SdKfz76	Observation balloon cable carrier
SdKfz77	Telephone cable
SdKfz79	Workshop
SdKfz83	Searchlight
SdKfz92	Personnel decontamination
SdKfz93	Clothing decontamination
SdKfz94	Water tanker

SdKfz95	Stores
SdKfz301	Radio antenna
SdKfz302	Radio
SdKfz303	Interceptor
SdKfz305	Cargo, closed body
SdKfz317	Oxygen tank
SdKfz354	Photographic
SdKfz384	Aircraft fuel tanker
SdKfz384	Aircraft fuel tanker

SdKfz410	Anti-aircraft unit
SdKfz415	Anti-aircraft survey

Numbers above '300' were for *Luftwaffe* vehicles. The use of these codes was abandoned in 1943.

Following the occupation of Czechoslovakia and France, the *Wehrmacht* seized large numbers of medium-weight Praga, Tatra, Skoda and Renault trucks.

Left: A Steel-bodied 3-ton Canadian Military Pattern 4x4 general-service cargo truck. These vehicles were constructed on Chevrolet (C60L) or Ford (F60L) chassis. The same chassis was also converted to the stores or light machinery role. *(ST)*

Right: The German-built Ford G917T was the forerunner of the V3000S and was based on the equivalent US-built Ford of 1939. Power was provided by a 3,600cc, and subsequently a 3,900cc, V8 petrol engine. There was also an open-cab variant and production continued until 1941. *(UB)*

Der Generalin[p
für das
deutsche Straßen
Nr.836

WH
OT

Above: A commercial Ford G917T 3-ton truck with a wood-mounted gas producer plant behind the cab. Many civilian - and, for that matter, military - vehicles were forced to run on producer gas because of the shortage of petrol. *(UB)*

Right: The open-cabbed Krupp L3H163 was a medium off-road truck dating from the mid-1930s. Most were fitted with a cargo/troop carrier body. The vehicle is part of a transport column entering Salzburg at the annexation of Austria, 12 March 1938. *(UB)*

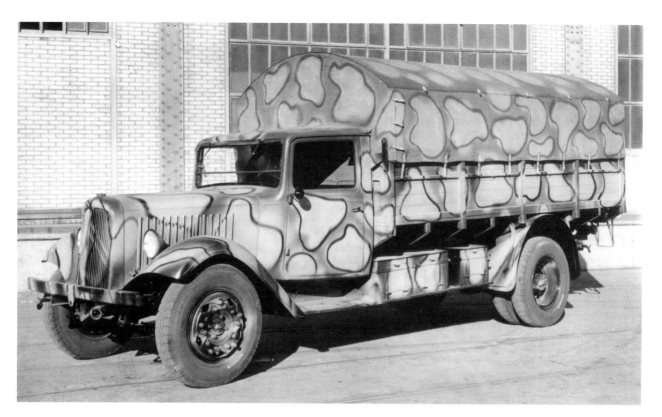

Above: An unusually camouflaged Citroën T45U 4x2 cargo truck. Introduced in 1934, this is typical of commandeered Citroëns used by the *Wehrmacht* after 1940. *(PW)*

Left: 3-ton 4x2 Opel Blitz with the so-called *Koffer* or house body which was used for a variety of roles, including signals and ambulance. *(PW)*

Above: German Ford V3000S showing the result of all of the shortages of materials. It is powered by a wood-gas producer plant and is fitted with simplified front mudguards and an *Einheits* cab. *(JSS)*

Right: Introduced in 1939, the British-built Commer Q4 was one of the less numerous 3-ton 4x2 general-service cargo vehicles used in military service. *(IWM)*

Great Britain

The 3-ton truck was the prime military transport for the British Army during World War Two, with more than 390,000 examples in service by VE Day.

Most British truck manufacturers produced a vehicle of this type, many of them having pre-war origins, and there was no attempt made to adopt a standard design... or even to standardise any aspects of design. In the early years of the war, most of the 3-ton class were of the 4x2 configuration but all-wheel drive types started to appear in small numbers around 1941, notably from Albion, Austin, Bedford, Karrier, Ford and Thornycroft.

The Bedford OY and QL were probably the most successful of the 3-tonners, and were certainly the most numerous. Dating from 1939, with some 72,000 examples built, the OY was produced as the OYD, a rigid 4x2 chassis which could be bodied as a GS cargo vehicle, workshop, battery slave truck, stores and office. As the OYC chassis/cab it was most frequently equipped with a water tank. First appearing in 1941, the QL was a forward-control 4x4 design which was also built in quantity (52,250 between 1941 and 1945) and also equipped for a variety of roles,

including GS cargo, troop carrier, tipper, tanker, signals and gun tractor. Both the OY and the QL were powered by a six-cylinder petrol engine of 3,519cc, coupled to a four-speed gearbox.

Many pre-war 6x4 3-ton also remained in production during the early years of World War Two, notably designs produced by AEC, Albion, Crossley, Guy, Leyland and Thornycroft; some were petrol powered, others were fitted diesel engines which cannot have helped with the logistics of delivering and storing fuel. Other types appeared later in the war, including Ford's

Top: A 3-ton Albion FT11N 4x4 cargo truck. Approximately 500 were produced from 1940. *(TM)*

Above: A total of 52,000 examples of the 3-ton Bedford QL were produced between 1941 and 1945. Most were bodied as GS cargo vehicles but there were also tractors for semi-trailer. *(TM)*

Above: A 3-ton Austin K3, 4x2 cargo truck. Production started in 1939 and continued until 1945; early vehicles had open cabs. *(ST)*

Right: The Bedford OYD was the most numerous of the 3-ton British 4x2 cargo trucks and was equipped for a variety of roles. More than 72,000 were delivered before production was halted in 1945. *(ST)*

Left: A Bedford QLR signals vehicle finished in post-war gloss Deep Bronze Green. Many of these vehicles remained in service for a further 10 or 15 years after the end of World War Two. *(ST)*

Below: A 3-ton Thornycroft Nubian. Nearly 4,000 of these 3-ton 4x4 general service trucks were built from mid-1940, most of which were supplied to the RAF *(ST)*.

Right: Albion FT11N 3-ton 4x4 GS cargo truck with the tilt reduced in height to lower the profile of the vehicle. *(TM)*

Right: Bedford QLC tractor and 6-ton semi-trailer. The Tasker-type coupling between the tractor and trailer was not readily detachable and the vehicle was referred to as a 4x4-2. *(TM)*

Right: A 3-ton Canadian Military Pattern (CMP) Ford F60H 6x4; the vehicle was unusual in being of three-axle layout but with a non-driving axle rearmost. *(TM)*

Left: A Thornycroft Nubian 4x4, bodied as a GS cargo vehicle. Approximately 5,000 of these trucks were built from 1940, with production continuing after the end of World War Two. *(PW)*

Left: A 3-ton Thornycroft ZS 4x2 generator/ water tank. An electricity generator was sited directly in front of and powered by the engine directly; the water tank was carried behind the cab. The vehicle was used by the RAF as part of a photographic processing unit. *(PW)*

Left: A 3-ton Leyland Retriever WLW 6x4 GS cargo vehicle. Essentially a pre-war design, the Retriever remained in production throughout the war with some 6,500 produced for a variety of roles. *(PW)*

Right: A column of 3-ton Albion BY5 6x4 trucks equipped with the folding boat body, No. 1, Mk II, for use as part of a bridging unit. The vehicle was produced from 1941 to 1945. *(IWM)*

Above: A 3-ton Thornycroft WZ 4x2 cargo vehicle. Little more than a lightly-militarised Sturdy chassis, the WZ was also produced with a short wheelbase for use as a three-way tipper vehicle. *(PW)*

WOT1, a 3-ton 6x4 dating from 1940. Also the Austin K6, which dated from as late as 1944.

There were also numbers of commercial trucks pressed into military service, notable amongst them were the 3-ton Ford E917T 6x4 and the Dodge 4x2 Models 80 and 82, built at the company's Kew, south London, assembly plant.

Large numbers of basically-commercial 3 ton pre-war trucks were also supplied direct to the British War Office by Canadian and US manufacturers, and the British Army also received many 2¹/₂ ton trucks of US origin, including GMCs and Studebakers, under the Lend-Lease program.

Italy

The Italian War Ministry had laid down specifications for standardised medium (and heavy) military trucks in the mid-1930s. Described as *autocarro unificato medio* (abbreviated to AUM, or simply CM), these medium trucks were designed to carry a payload up to 3 tonnes (6,614lb), with a gross vehicle weight not exceeding 6.5 tonnes (14,330lb), and a top speed of 40mph (60km/h).

Alfa-Romeo, Bianchi, Fiat, SPA, Isotta-Fraschini, Lancia and OM all supplied standardised medium trucks but, in practice, there was little attempt at real standardisation. Civilian trucks were frequently modified to meet the Ministry's performance standard. Both petrol and diesel engines were used, occasionally with these alternatives offered in the same basic chassis but unlike most nations, the majority of Italian Army trucks were diesel powered; some were of forward-control design, others were bonneted. There was just one 4x4 design in this category, the 2¹/₂ ton SPA T-40 truck which was based on the similar artillery tractor, although it must be noted

that the SPA Dovunque series offered good cross-country performance, particularly the 6x6 Tipo 41.

Standard bodies included cargo, tanker and workshop, there were also a number of specialised vehicles.

Aside from the *unificato* designs, the Italian Army also used large numbers of older trucks from Fiat, Lancia and SPA.

Japan

Although the Japanese truck industry had been under pressure to produce military vehicles in the late 1930s, during World War Two there were just two types of domestic medium truck in military service.

The Isuzu TU10 was a civilian 3 ton 6x4 truck which first appeared in 1934, and which subsequently evolved into the military 2-ton Type 94 (see page 26). The TU23 was an updated version which entered production in 1941.

Soviet Union

The Soviet Union received more than 200,000 US-built medium trucks under the Lend-Lease program, mostly of the 6x6 and 6x4 Studebaker US6 type, as well as large numbers of British and Canadian-built vehicles.

Home-grown 2 to 3 ton medium trucks were of decidedly pre-war commercial design, and were generally derived from US truck practice of the late 1920s. Although there were several designs, offering 4x2, 4x4 and 6x4 drive-lines, rated at $2^1/_4$, $2^1/_2$ and 3 tons, all were produced by the Moscow-based ZIS plant from 1933, and all were powered by the same 5,522cc six-cylinder side-valve petrol engine; the 3-ton 4x4 ZIS-5V was also subsequently produced in the Ulyanovsk and Miass plants. Various body types were used, including cargo, searchlight, bridging equipment, air compressor and tanker.

A number of halftracks were also based on

Top: An Italian-built 3-ton OM Taurus cargo truck; the type N was diesel and the type B petrol powered. The type C was a 'colonial' model. *(AN)*

Above: An Austin K5 chassis of the British Army 3-ton 4x4, of which some 12,280 were supplied between 1941 and 1945. Most were bodied as GS cargo vehicles, but this example is fitted with a communications body. *(IWM)*

the ZIS-22 and 42 chassis using Somua-type tracks. Although the vehicles were relatively crude, being little more than conversions of the ZIS wheeled trucks, more than 5,000 examples were produced in four variants.

United States of America

US Army medium trucks tended to be either militarised $2\frac{1}{2}$ or 3-ton vehicles, generally derived from civilian 4x2 trucks of the late 1930s, or standardised military heavy-duty $2\frac{1}{2}$ ton 6x4 and 6x6 models, both of which were able to withstand more than 100% overloading when used on the road. The $2\frac{1}{2}$ ton 6x6 was the most widely used transport truck of the war, and was generally considered to be the 'workhorse' truck. More than 800,000 were produced. Note that for light and medium trucks, the US tended to exclusively use petrol engines.

Most important and numerous of the standardised $2\frac{1}{2}$ ton class was the GMC CCKW, a

Above: The GMC
CCKW was not the
only US-built
2¹/₂-ton 6x6 truck.
Studebaker also built
some 200,000
vehicles of this type,
designated US6,
most of which went
to the Soviet Union
under Lend-Lease.
(PW)

bonnetted 6x6 design derived from the company's pre-war ACKWX-353, and produced in two wheelbase lengths; the CCKW-352, measuring up at 145in (3.68m) and the CCKW-353 with a 164in (4.17m) wheelbase. Both were powered by a 4,416cc General Motors six-cylinder overhead-valve petrol engine producing 104bhp. This drove all wheels through a five-speed manual transmission and two-speed transfer case; drive to the front axle could be disengaged when not required. A number of vehicles were fitted with a front-mounted winch. Early vehicles were fitted with an all-steel civilian-type closed cab, but this was subsequently superseded by an open-cab design which enabled a lower profile to be achieved in the field and also reduced shipping height. Most CCKW chassis were equipped with a steel personnel/cargo body, but other variants included compressor, dump, water fuel tanker, workshop, high-lift van, bomb service, pontoon bridge truck and stake truck. A small number were also fitted with wooden cargo bodies. The total number of

Left: A 3-ton Leyland Retriever 6x4 chassis equipped with a photographic processing body. *(PW)*

Right: One of a great number of well restored GMC CCKW-353 vehicles which travel the miltary shows. *(ST)*

Left: Colloquially-known as either the 'Deuce and a Half' or 'Jimmy', the $2\frac{1}{2}$-ton 6x6 GMC CCKW was one of the vehicles which helped to win the war. The truck was used by all of the Allies and by all arms of service and formed the backbone of the US Army's supply chain. The vehicle shown is being loaded onto a LCT at Weymouth, Dorset in preparation for the D-Day landings on 6 June 1944. *(UB)*

Left: Another well restored GMC CCKW-353 of the variant fitted with a front winch. *(ST)*

Right: A 3-ton Bedford OYC 4x2 water tanker showing the tubular framework which allowed the vehicle to be disguised as a GS cargo truck. The OY was the most common 3-ton 4x2 in the British Army, with almost 72,500 built during the war years. *(PW)*

CCKW trucks produced between 1941 and 1945 was 562,750.

Note: ACKWX: A: 1939 design; C: conventional cab; K: front-wheel drive; W: tandem rear drive; X: non-standard wheelbase; ie. different from any civilian model; 353: 164in wheelbase; 352: 145in wheelbase. CCKW: C : 1941.

The GMC CCW-353 was an otherwise similar 6x4 chassis on which the low gears of the transfer case were blocked.

Similar $2^1/_2$-ton vehicles included the Studebaker US6, which was also produced in both 6x6 and 6x4 configuration. The International K5 was supplied mainly to the US Marine Corps, but in much smaller numbers.

The Federal 2G and 3G models were unusual in being $2^1/_2$-ton trucks of military pattern with two axles and rear-wheel drive only; the company also produced a $3^1/_2$-ton tractor truck (designated 3G) using the same engine and drive train.

A steel-bodied Chevrolet 3-ton cargo vehicle, Model YS4103, was produced for the British using a Thornton bogie at the rear to allow a 6x4 drive.

Right: More than 13,000 of these 3-ton Austin K6 6x4 vehicles were produce, many of which were used by the RAF, as this example fitted as a mobile office. *(PW)*

Above: A US-supplied Studebaker US6 being used as an artillery tractor by the Red Army. *(PW)*

Left: A 2¹/₂-ton Autocar U8144-T 4x4 tractor unit together with a US Army Air Corps 2,000-gallon fuel-servicing semi-trailer. Some 550 examples were produced between 1940 and 1941. *(PW)*

Left: A Long-wheelbase 3-ton Canadian Military pattern (CMP) 4x4 equipped with a British-type drop-side GS cargo body. Almost 25% of the CMP chassis produced during the war years were of the 3-ton class. *(TM)*

4 | Heavy Trucks over 3 tons

Heavy trucks of the period included an enormous variety of vehicles from dozens of manufacturers, with load capacities ranging from 4 tons up to 10, or even 12 tons, and with 4x2, 4x4, 6x4 and 6x6 drive. Many in this category were basically road-going civilian machines which were pressed into military service, including numbers of tractors designed for use with semi-trailers.

Purpose-designed military vehicles with all-wheel drive became more numerous from about 1941, most notably after the US entered the war. The need for reliability and improved performance, particularly load-carrying performance, inevitably pushed truck technology forward, and the heavy trucks of 1945 bore little relation to many of the primitive pre-war designs with which, for example, Britain and Germany entered the conflict. Aside from the US-built trucks which were generally petrol-powered, often requiring capacities up to 12,000cc or 14,000cc, diesel engines started to become the standard unit for heavy trucks and technological improvements were rapid. The Czech company Tatra, for example, produced 12,000cc V8 and 14,800cc V12 air-cooled diesels for use in the 6, 8 and 10-ton capacity all-wheel-drive designs.

Again with the exception of Tatra, which employed an innovative swing-axle design to achieve independent suspension to all wheels, little true progress was made in suspension design with most trucks continuing to be fitted with live axles suspended on multi-leaf, semi-elliptical springing. Driver comfort was not considered to be of any importance, but at least power-assisted steering and brakes began to be fitted as standard equipment even if the braking systems were sometimes of the mechanical type. Pneumatic tyres had been a customary fitment even for heavy trucks since the beginning of the 1930s and had become very reliable but, even so, some Italian truck designs retained solid or semi-solid tyres until the end of World War Two.

If there is a vehicle design which can be identified as being the most significant, it would probably be the US-built forward-control Autocar 4x2 and 4x4 or International 4x2 tractor units, in the 5 to 6 ton class, which were intended to be used with a 12-ton gross weight semi-trailer. Both vehicle designs anticipated the post-war trend for articulated heavy trucks using a standardised fifth-wheel coupling. The German Mercedes-Benz LG4500 is also worth

Left: A 4^1/$_2$-ton Mercedes-Benz L4500A 4x4 heavy cargo truck in *Luftwaffe* service being unloaded from a transport ship in a North African port, 1 October 1941. These trucks were built between 1941 and 1944; there was also a 4x2 variant. Both types were also built under licence by Saurer in Austria. *(UB)*

Above: Built in Czechoslovakia, the 5-ton Tatra T85 and T85A 6x4 was much favoured by the *Wehrmacht*. Variants included cargo vehicles, and fuel tankers. The vehicle is part of a motorised column entering Breslau, 9 September 1940. *(UB)*

Right: The 9-ton German Faun L900 was mainly used as a tank carrier but the open-type body also aloowed other heavy load-carrying duties. Introduced in 1938, the vehicle was produced with either a Deutz 6 or 8-cylinder diesel engine. The vehicles are part of the grand parade for Hitlers 50th birthday, 20 April 1939. *(UB)*

noting since it remained in production for commercial users into the post-war years.

It is also worth noting that many of these vehicles were capable of being considerably overloaded (as much as 100%) particularly when all-wheel-drive cross-country types of vehicle were used on the road.

Canada

A long-wheelbase version of the Diamond T, known as Model 975A, was produced specially for the Canadian Army. Built in the US, only the body was manufactured in Canada. Many of these vehicles saw service with the British Army.

Germany

In Germany, a 'heavy' truck was one rated at more than 4 tons, and the Schell Programme divided these vehicles into two categories: Type S trucks with 4x2 drive intended for use on the road, and the 4x4 Type ' (*Allradantrieb* - all-wheel drive) trucks. However, most heavy truck production was of Type S vehicles.

Standardisation was not generally apparent in the procurement of heavy trucks, most being lightly-militarised vehicles of civilian origin, and almost all were diesel-engined. Indeed, as the war continued, many different types were pressed into service which must have caused logistical problems in training and the procurement of parts. All German truck manufacturers were involved, as well as Tatra and Skoda in Czechoslovakia. In Austria the Saurer company also manufactured the Mercedes-Benz L4500. After the occupation of France in 1940 Renault 5 and 6-ton trucks were also procured in large numbers and, of course, the *Wehrmacht* was perfectly happy to operate captured vehicles.

The most successful of the myriad types in service was the diesel-engined Mercedes-Benz L4500, produced as a 4x4 (L4500A) and 4x2 (L4500S). Introduced in 1939, the vehicle was a conventional bonneted truck featuring a modern-looking all-steel cab. Both types were fitted with a hybrid air/hydraulic braking system. In total some 11,000 were produced, of which 3,000 were the 4x4 variant. There was even a halftrack (*maultier* - mule) conversion of this

Above: The Fiat 665NM or 666N 4x2 heavy cargo truck was produced between 1942 and 1944. The types were similar in appearance, differing primarily in wheelbase length. This Italian Army motor column is on the East front, 1 June 1942. *(UB)*

Top: The 10-ton AEC Model O854 6x6 was derived from the company's 4x4 Matador. Most were equipped as 2,000/2,500-gallon aircraft refuelling tankers. *(RAFM)*

Above: The same chassis was also fitted with various body types such as: mobile crane, armoured command, and oxygen/nitrogen producing variants. *(PW)*

chassis, designated the LG4500R. One type was fitted with the track and bogie system from a Panzer II light tank. Another type was fitted with a lighter track system mounted on semi-elliptical springs.

The Büssing-NAG 500 and the 4500 model and also the MAN ML4500 trucks were similar with both types produced in 4x2 and 4x4 variants. Some 15,000 Büssing-NAGs were built, whilst examples of the MAN were also constructed by ÖAF (Österreichische Automobil-Fabriks) in Vienna, Austria.

Jointly designed by KHD (Klöckner-Humboldt-Deutz), Henschel and Saurer, the

GS145 (*Gemeinschaftsfahrgestell*) was the closest vehicle to a standardised two-axle heavy truck in German Army service. However only small numbers were produced, all by KHD.

Of the larger 6x4 and 6x6 trucks, aside from the 6x4 German-built Faun L900D567, most were of Czech origin, the largest being the 6x6 Tatra T111. This vehicle was powered by a 14,825cc V12 air-cooled diesel engine and was available with different, independent suspension systems to suit 6$\frac{1}{2}$ or 8-ton loads.

Great Britain

As with the other types of truck, necessity forced the British Army to use a ragbag of designs, including many essentially pre-war domestic trucks and lightly-militarised commercial vehicles alongside many vehicles of US origin.

A splendid 10-ton class 6x6 military chassis was produced by AEC mainly for use as an aircraft refuelling tanker. Although the vehicle was initially fitted with a petrol engine, from 1942 this was replaced by the company's own 7,700cc A187 diesel engine. Both 2,000 gallon (9,092 litre) and 2,500 gallon (11,365 litre) versions were produced.

Albion, Leyland and Foden also supplied diesel-powered 10-ton class vehicles, generally

derived from their pre-war commercial models. Leyland's 10-ton 6x4 Hippo was the most successful and long-lived British designed GS cargo vehicle in this weight category; the Mk I was a pre-war design fitted with an open cab but the Mk II and Mk IIB, which appeared in 1944, were fitted with an all-steel enclosed cab and a more-powerful 7,400cc six-cylinder water-cooled diesel engine. More than 1,000 examples were constructed and the Hippo remained in service into the 1950s.

At the lighter end of the category, Bedford's 5 and 6 ton OW, OXC and QLC 4x4 models were all powered by the company's own 3,519cc six-cylinder water-cooled petrol engine. The OXC and QLC were tractor units designed for use with either a Tasker or Scammell semi-trailer.

Typical of the 6 ton-class GS cargo vehicles were the Maudslay Militant, Dennis Max, Foden DG4/6 and ERF 2CI4. The Militant dated from 1940 and was powered by a 5,541cc Gardner 4LW water-cooled diesel engine; around 700 examples were produced for the Royal Army Service Corps. The Dennis, ERF and Foden vehicles were militarised versions of commercial types and all were diesel powered.

Similarly, trucks supplied by Fordson and Commer were based on each company's standard production commercial vehicles.

Italy

As with the medium (*medio*) trucks, the Italian War Ministry had laid down specifications for standardised heavy vehicles in the mid-1930s which were designated as *autocarro unificato pesante* (AUP, or CP). The specification was admirably loose, with a heavy truck defined as one capable of carrying a payload of 6 tonnes (13,228lb), with a gross vehicle weight not exceeding 12 tonnes (26,457lb), and a top speed of 28mph (45km/h), or 24mph (38km/h) when towing a 12 tonne (26,457lb) trailer.

Above: Foden DG6/10 chassis equipped with a fixed-side 10-ton cargo body. Several hundred were constructed between 1939 and 1941 for road-going duties. Later models used single rear wheels. (TM)

Left: The 'Queen Mary' trailer, was a 3-ton low-loader design intended for moving aircraft and aircraft components. Manufacturered by Taskers of Andover, it is seen here coupled to a 6-ton Bedford OXC tractor unit. *(PW)*

Left: A Commer Q2 tractor unit coupled to a 'Queen Mary' recovery trailer. The Bedford OXC (above), the Commer and the trailer were produced from 1939. The trailer was used by the RAF and RN for many years after World War Two. *(PW)*

Above: A 10-ton Leyland Hippo Mk II 6x4 cargo vehicle. First produced in late 1944, the Mk II remained in production into the 1950s. *(ST)*

Right: The US Army's 4-5 ton Autocar U-7144T 4x4 tractor for semi-trailer use was typical of the road-going vehicles used in the supply chain role. Production started in 1941 and continued until 1945; similar vehicles were also constructed by White (designated 444T). *(ST)*

Above: A 6-ton Mack NM 6x6 cargo vehicle. Most of the 7,000 built went to the Allies under Lend-Lease. Four variants were in production from 1942 until 1945, NM5, NM6, NM7 and NM8, differing only in detail. (ST)

Left: A 4-5 ton Federal 94X43A tractor for semi-trailers. Both open and closed cab versions were built. The trailer is a 12-ton Fruehauf van as used by anti-aircraft artillery units to house radio equipment. (ST)

Most of Italy's truck manufacturers produced heavy trucks for the Italian Army, including Alfa Romeo, Breda, Fiat, SPA, Isotta Fraschini and Lancia. All were diesel powered and, whilst most were produced as cargo vehicles, there were also examples bodied for the tanker, wrecker, workshop and other special roles.

Of note are the Alfa Romeo 800RE, a particularly-modern looking forward-control 4x2 truck, which was also produced as an experimental half-track, and the SPA Dovunque 41, a 5 to 6-ton 6x6 bonneted truck with a 9,300cc SPA six-cylinder water-cooled diesel engine, lockable axle differentials, five-speed gearbox and two-speed transfer case. Both of these designs remained in production until around 1950. The latter Dovunque was also produced as an artillery tractor.

Below: A 7½-ton Federal 606 tractor unit coupled to an aircraft refuelling tanker. *(PW)*

Fiat produced several 4x2 heavy trucks of both bonnetted and forward-control pattern, early examples of which retained solid tyres.

Dating from the mid-1930s, the Isotta Fraschini D80MO was another very modern 4x2 heavy cargo truck, powered by the company's 7,200cc water-cooled diesel engine, and fitted with a five-speed gearbox and a differential lock in the rear axle. The D80MO was superseded by the D80COM in 1939.

Japan

Heavy trucks used by the Japanese Imperial Army included the 7-ton Isuzu TB60, a diesel-engined 4x2 cargo vehicle dating from 1941, and the 20-ton Isuzu TH10 6x4 dump truck of 1943. The TB60 remained in production after the war whilst the TH10, a massive machine for the period with a hydraulically-operated 424cu/ft (12cu/m) capacity steel body, was built only in small numbers. The Imperial Navy intended to use the TB60 for dock construction and similar work.

Soviet Union

The Soviet Union had just two domestic heavy trucks – the YaG-10 and YaG-12 – both produced by the Yaroslavl Automobile Plant and powered by a 7,020cc six-cylinder petrol engine of US origin.

Of these, the 12-ton YaG-12 an 8x8 vehicle fitted with a US-designed Continental engine, was the heaviest and the more interesting. It was in production from 1932 to 1941 although the numbers produced were limited.

Rated at 8 tons, and also in production between 1932 and 1941, the YaG-10 was powered by a US-designed 7,020cc Hercules YXC engine.

United States of America

The US has always had a strong tradition of heavy truck manufacture, with companies such as Autocar, White, Diamond T, Sterling, Corbitt and others effectively custom-building trucks to suit particular applications.

Amongst standardised types the 4-ton Diamond T 6x6 is typical. First appearing in 1941, the Diamond T was supplied in various models equipped for different roles including cargo and prime mover, flat bed, dump, water tanker, machinery, bitumen tanker, bridging pontoon and air compressor. Like many of these heavy trucks it was powered by an engine from an outside source, in this case the 8,669cc Hercules RXB or RXC six-cylinder water-cooled petrol engine. The long wheelbase Model 975 and 975A, were only built for the Canadian Army.

Autocar produced a number of 5 to 6-ton tractor units, some of which were also powered by the Hercules RXC engine for use with 12-ton gross weight semi-trailers. Similar vehicles were also produced by International, Kenworth, Marmon-Herrington and Federal.

The products of the Mack Brothers Company of Allentown, Pennsylvania are worth detailing since not only did the company build some fine heavyweight trucks but, unusually amongst the companies in this market sector, they tended to use engines of the company's own design. Among the largest of the vehicles was the NR series, a 10-ton cargo type dating from 1940 and powered by the company's 8,505cc Lanova six-cylinder water-cooled diesel engine; more than 16,500 examples

Right: An Italian 6-ton Alfa-Romeo 800RE 4x2 cargo truck, built between 1940 and 1944. (AN)

were completed before production ceased in 1945. The petrol-engined NM series was a 6-ton 6x6 design used both as a cargo vehicle and as a prime mover for anti-aircraft guns. Trucks from the 5-ton semi-forward control petrol-engined EHU and EHUT series were supplied to Britain in 1942 as part of the Lend-Lease program; also rated at 5 tons was the EH series, a militarised commercial vehicle which was supplied in large numbers (almost 3,500 between 1943 and 1945) as a cargo truck and tractor unit.

Largest of all was the massive Mack FCSW 30-ton dump truck, a number of which were acquired by the British Ministry of Works.

The 6-ton White Model 666 was a 6x6 cargo/prime mover fitted with various body types including a workshop van and tanker. The 666 was also produced to the same specification by Corbitt. A total of over 21,000 were produced by both companies.

The Corbitt SD series were 6, 8 and 10-ton 6x4 and 6x6, heavy tractors designed for use with a semi-trailer. The vehicles were basically a commercial type intended for long-distance freight haulage.

The 6x4 Federal 604 and 6x4 Reo 28XS tractors were intended for hauling engineers' plant, but were also supplied to the British with a Trailmobile semi-trailer suitable for use as a 20-ton tank transporter.

Most curious in this class is probably the Ford/E&L Transport twin-engined 6x4 truck built in 1940 to transport components for

Consolidated Liberator and other aircraft from Ford's aircraft factories at Tulsa, Oklahoma and Fort Worth, Texas to the assembly plant at Willow Run. Two 7,834cc V8 petrol engines were installed side-by-side, each driving one of the rear axles through a four-speed gearbox. Some 100 of these unique vehicles were built, together with special 63ft (19m) double-deck semi-trailers, two of which could carry the component parts (excluding the engines) to build a Liberator bomber. The trucks were run around the clock with drivers alternating in five-hour shifts. Some examples were fitted with sleeper cabs.

Lesser-known companies such as Biederman, Brockway, FWD, Corbitt and Hug also produced modest numbers of heavy-duty 6 to 18 ton-class trucks.

Top: A US-built Federal 604 6x4 tractor for a 20-ton semi-trailer. Powered by a Cummins HB600 diesel engine, around 1,500 of these vehicles were built between 1942 and 1944, mainly for Lend-Lease; 450 came to Britain. *(PW)*

Above: A 10-ton Brockway dump truck as supplied to the Ministry of Supply during early World War Two. *(TM)*

Right: Although designed as a 6-ton cargo truck, the Mack NM was also used as a tank transporter tractor. These are coupled to 45-ton Rogers trailers and are loaded with new Comet tanks from the Leyland Motors factory in Lancashire in 1944. *(PW)*

Left: Some 100 of these Ford/E&L Transport 6x4 tractors were built in 1940 to transport components for Consolidated Liberator and other aircraft from Ford's factories at Tulsa and Fort Worth to the assembly plant at Willow Run. Two of the special 63-foot long double-deck semi-trailers could carry all of the components of a Liberator bomber except the engines. *(PW)*

Left: The Commer Q6 Superpoise, was produced in large numbers for the RN. Rated at 6 tons and with rear-wheel drive only, this was essentially a commercial truck used by the military. *(PW)*

Below: The 10-ton White 760 4x2 truck was used by the British Army as a tank carrier. Similar vehicles were also used for transporting aircraft. The tank is a Mk IV cruiser, which weighed almost 15 tons! *(TM)*

Left: Prototype Mack NO4 heavy recovery vehicle. Two examples of this vehicle were built in December 1942, one for the US Army Air Force, the other for the US Navy. The Gar Wood recovery equipment was similar to that fitted to the standardised M1A1 heavy wreckers. A fifth-wheel coupling allowed the truck to be used with a semi-trailers. *(TM)*

Below: The 8-ton Corbitt 40SD6 6x4 tractor unit was designed to be used with a heavy semi-trailer for long-distance road haulage. *(TM)*

5 | Tractors and Prime Movers

Wheeled, tracked and half-tracked prime movers, gun portees (these were peculiar to the British and Commonwealth Armies), tank transporters, and wheeled and tracked tractors, and nowhere are the different approaches of the various combatants illustrated better than in their attitude to these types of vehicle.

The word tractor is defined in the Oxford English Dictionary as a 'self-propelled vehicle for hauling other vehicles, machinery, etc'... whilst the US Department of Defense defines a prime mover as 'a vehicle, including heavy construction equipment, possessing military characteristics, designed primarily for towing heavy, wheeled weapons and frequently providing facilities for the transportation of the crew of, and ammunition for, the weapon'.

In practice, such vehicles may take the form of a wheeled truck intended for towing either a gun or a draw-bar trailer; a modified agricultural machine, typically intended for towing artillery or aircraft; or a specialised heavy tracked or half-tracked vehicle specifically for use as a heavy artillery tractor. Purpose-designed tank transporters are also included here, regardless of whether they are rigid-chassis tank carriers, tractor-trucks designed for use with a dedicated semi-trailer, or ballast tractors.

Note that the US Army also used the term 'tractor' to describe tractor-trucks intended for use with a semi-trailer, but these have been covered in the 'truck' sections under the appropriate weight.

Germany

Although the German Army did not have any purpose-designed tank transporters similar to British or US vehicles types, preferring to transport tanks by rail over long distances, there were plenty of standardised half-track vehicles intended for towing. Designed in the mid-1930s, these well-engineered vehicles were expensive and time-consuming to produce, ranging from the 1-ton SdKfz10, through 8, 10 and 12-ton classifications, up to the massive 18-ton Famo SdKfz 9; a 'light' prime mover was rated at up to 3 tons, 'medium' vehicles were rated at 5 to 8 tons, and 'heavy' prime movers were in the range 12 to 18 tons.

All were designed to be used either as prime movers for artillery, or as heavy equipment

Above: The US Army's heaviest tractor of World War Two was the 12-ton M26 6x6 produced by Pacific Car & Foundry and dubbed the 'Dragon Wagon'. Powered by a huge Hall Scott petrol engine, the vehicle was produced in both armoured (seen here) and soft-skin forms. *(ST)*

Left: An M26 with armoured shields in place protecting the crew compartment. The vehicle is towing a Sherman medium tank equipped with wading gear. *(JSS)*

Above: German tanks (Panzer Is) were frequently carried in trucks such as these 9-ton Faun L900 6x4 cargo/tank carriers. Dating from the late 1930s, and powered by a Deutz diesel engine, the truck was essentially a militarised commercial vehicle. *(UB)*

Right: The Demag D7 (Sd.Kfz.10) was originally intended as a tractor for light artillery. *(UB)*

transporters in conjunction with a suitable low-loading or special trailer adapted to carry a tank, rocket rcfuelling equipment, or used as a gun mount. It was not uncommon for even the larger tractors to be used in tandem. The standard tank-transporter trailer was a 60-ton eight-wheeled design (TiefldAnhFPzKpfw.642) with a removable rear bogie to facilitate loading, and was steered (assisted with air piston-type servos) at the both the front and rear.

Aside from the motorcycle-based *Kettenkrad*, which was powered by a 1,478cc Opel Olympic four-cylinder water-cooled petrol engine and built exclusively by NSU, all the standardised halftrack vehicles were designed to be built by more than one manufacturer to a common

design. Maybach engines were used in all weight categories, the smaller vehicles being fitted with the 3,790cc or 4,170cc six-cylinder water-cooled petrol engine. The 8-ton medium SdKfz 7 was equipped with a 6,191cc six-cylinder unit while the 12 and 18-ton variants used a 7,973cc or 10,838cc V12 water-cooled petrol engine respectively. The SdKfz 6 was also built in Czechoslovakia by Praga, and a low-cost version, the sWS, (*schwereWehrmachtShclepper* - heavy army tractor) was produced by Tatra from 1943.

Various heavy wheeled tractors were also produced by the likes of Kaelble, Hanomag and Faun, both for use as aircraft tractors by the *Luftwaffe*, and for road work in conjunction

Below: Largest of the German half-tracks was the FAMO F2 (Sd.Kfz.9), an 18-ton monster which was used to tow artillery and engineers' equipment as well as being used as a tank transporter or retriever. (*UB*)

Above: The Gardner-powered Scammell Pioneer was produced in recovery, artillery tractor and tank-transporter variants. This is the 30-ton TRMU30, a tractor intended for use with a purpose-built semi-trailer (TRCU30) as a tank transporter. Although well thought of by crews, the Pioneer was never available in suffiicient numbers and became increasingly obsolete as tanks became heavier. (ST)

Right: The Albion FT15N was a low-profile field artillery tractor produced in small numbers (approximately 150) during 1945. (ST)

Above: Morris-Commercial C8 field artillery tractor with the late pattern squared-off body introduced in 1944. A typical load for these tractors was the British 17- or 25-pounder field gun on a two-wheeled carriage, together with a two-wheeled ammunition limber. *(ST)*

Left: The earlier C8 model had a distinctive sloping back to the body. *(ST)*

Above: Built to a common pattern by Chevrolet and Ford, the Canadian Military Pattern (CMP) vehicles were probably the most successful attempt at standardisation in World War Two. Shown is the Ford FGT 4x4 field artillery tractor. (PW)

with a specialised draw-bar trailer. The largest of these was the Deutz-engined Faun ZR ballast tractor, which could tow a 40-ton trailer; the Faun ZRS (Schienenzepp conversion) variant was designed for use on rails as a shunter and prime mover for rail wagons.

The large-wheeled *Radschlepper, Ost* (wheeled tractor - East) – often abbreviated to simply *Radschlepper* – was designed by Ferdinand Porsche specifically for use as an artillery tractor on the Eastern Front where conditions were often very severe, and some 200 were built by Skoda in Czechoslovakia. Similar in design, was the French-built Latil FTARH, an Eastern Front version of the company's TARH tractor, which could tow up to 40 tons (40,642Kg) and which was produced for the German Army during the time that Latil was controlled by Mercedes-Benz. French Laffly tractors were also pressed into service.

The Czech-built Skoda 6K was used as a tank carrier, specifically for the Skoda LT35 light tank, but it was equally suitable for any small AFVs up to 11 tons in weight. The 9-ton Büssing-NAG 900 was also used as a carrier for light tanks.

Great Britain

As regards tank transporters, Britain entered the war with small numbers of the 20-ton Scammell Pioneer TRMU-20 tractor/semi-trailer combination, plus a variety of rigid-chassis trucks, from US manufacturers Mack, White and White-Ruxtall, which were suitable for tanks up to approximately 18 tons (18,289Kg). The Scammell was subsequently upgraded to 30 tons (30,482Kg) and re-designated TRMU-30 and, although reliable, the Gardner-engined Pioneer was never available in sufficient numbers and also lacked the capability required for the increasingly heavy tanks which were produced as the war progressed. The 18-ton trucks were similarly unsatisfactory, and were soon rebodied and relegated to other duties.

Britain turned to the US for assistance and, from August 1941, was supplied with quantities of the Hercules diesel-engined Diamond T Model 980/981, a powerful, fine steel-bodied ballast tractor which could cope with a draw-bar load of up to 40 tons (40,642Kg) and which proved to be an extremely reliable vehicle. The differences between the models were minor, the

Model 980 was designed to use a winch only from the rear, whilst the Model 981 included fairlead rollers in the front bumper making it also suitable for retrieval work. Suitable multi-axle trailers were produced by Dyson, SMT, Shelvoke & Drury, Cranes and Hands in Great Britain, and by Fruehauf, Rogers, Pointer-Williamette and Winter-Weiss in the US. A number of Diamond T tractors were also converted for use with a 30-ton Shelvoke & Drury semi-trailer, similar to that used with the Scammell Pioneer.

Albion also supplied their CX24S tractor for tank transporter duties, but the engine and braking systems proved unreliable so the vehicle was downgraded to a 15-ton rating and relegated to carrying cable drums, telegraph poles and engineers' plant.

Four-wheel drive field artillery tractors (FAT) were supplied by Morris, Guy and Karrier in Great Britain, as well as from Ford and Chevrolet in Canada; all were intended to tow 17-pounder and 25-pounder field guns. An experimental low-silhouette light artillery tractor was also produced by Albion as the FT15N, but it arrived too late in the war to have much effect. The standard medium

artillery tractor was the diesel-powered AEC Matador 854, a 4x4 truck so tough and reliable that it was sometimes used as a stand-by tank transporter when coupled to an appropriate trailer. Heavy artillery tractors included the Albion CX22S and a longer-wheelbase version of the Scammell Pioneer known as the R100, replacing the earlier AEC 850 (formerly R6T); both vehicles provided accommodation for the gun crew and stowage and handling facilities for the

Right: The Scammell Pioneer R100 was the British Armies largest artillery tractor. Although lacking front-wheel drive, the slogging power of the Gardner 6LW diesel engine gave the vehicle superb haulage capacity. Approximately 780 examples were built between 1939 and 1945.*(ST)*

Below: The unique Scammell-designed pivoting and walking-beam suspension gave the formidable performance over rough terrain. *(PR)*

Above and left:
The *Wehrmacht* used large numbers of four-wheeled tractors in an attempt to cope with the appalling conditions on the Eastern Front.
This is a captured French-built Latil TARH, 4x4 tractor the development of which dated back to World War One.
The vehicle was evolved into the FTARH, a similar, solid-tyred tractor, developed especially for the German Army. *(UB)*

Above: In closed-cab form the Diamond T Model 980 (the 981 was similar but was equipped with fairlead roller in the front bumper) was one of the best-looking heavy trucks of the war. Although designed as a ballast tractor for tank-transporter trailers, it was versatile enough to be found hauling all kinds of oversized loads... in this case a Buffalo tracked landing vehicle. (LVT). *(IWM)*

Right: A Scammell Pioneer R100 artillery tractor in typical Blue and Sand camouflage of the Western Desert. The towed load is almost certainly a British 5.5inch howitzer. *(IWM)*

Above: Although production had ceased in 1936, a number of these venerable AEC/FWD R6T/850 6x6 artillery tractors remained in service with the British Expeditionary Force (BEF) in France in 1940. *(TM)*

ammunition. An underfloor winch was fitted for recovering the gun.

Gun portees were an exclusively British device, a light 4x4 truck designed to actually carry an artillery piece, typically a light field gun or anti-aircraft weapon, in such a way that it could be fired without being unloaded off the vehicle.

Airfield tractors were used for towing and recovering aircraft, and also for towing fuel bowsers and bomb trains; David Brown and Fordson both produced wheeled and tracked machines for these roles.

There were no British tracked vehicles of the type used by the US Army for towing heavy artillery.

Italy

Italian artillery tractors tended to be of wheeled design, often using large, solid- or semi-solid tyred wheels combined with four-wheel drive.

Most interesting of these is the Pavesi P4/100. Despite having first appeared in 1914,

the vehicle remained in production until 1942 in Italy and was licence-produced elsewhere. Originally running on dual solid tyres – these were replaced by pneumatics in 1938 – the vehicle was powered by a 4,724cc Pavesi four-cylinder water-cooled petrol engine and was steered by means of an articulation joint in the style of modern off-road plant.

The SPA TL37 and TM40 were both 4x4 designs with four-wheel steering; the former was bonneted, whilst the latter was of the characteristic Italian short-wheelbase forward-control layout, both featuring a lockable centre differential. Tyres on the TM40 were of semi-solid design.

The only really heavy artillery tractor was the 6x6 SPA Dovunque 41, a remarkably-modern design with a 9,365cc SPA six-cylinder water-cooled diesel engine, five-speed gearbox with a two-speed transfer case, lockable centre and axle differentials, and also air-assisted hydraulic brakes. The open body included seating for an 11-man gun crew.

Above: AEC Matador Model O853 medium artillery tractor struggling round a mountain pass. The tractor is towing the 3.7inch anti-aircraft gun on a four-wheeled carriage. *(TM)*

Breda produced solid-tyred heavy prime movers for the artillery and engineer roles; although somewhat 'veteran' in appearance, both featured 8,142cc four-cylinder water-cooled petrol engines driving all four wheels through a five-speed gearbox. Both types were fitted with differential locks.

Both Breda and Fiat also produced simplified versions of the SdKfz 7 half-tracks, numbers manufactured by Breda being supplied to the German Army.

Japan

In the late 1930s Isuzu and Ikegai produced 5 and 6-ton diesel-powered half-track tractors, using tank-type tracks, fitted with open rear bodies like the equivalent German vehicles. Both types were intended for use as prime movers for 75mm anti-aircraft guns.

From 1934, the Isuzu Type 94 6x4 medium truck was adapted as a wheeled artillery tractor, again intended to tow a 75mm anti-aircraft gun.

Right: The Hanomag SS100 4x2 heavy tractor. Produced between 1936 and 1944. The *Wehrmacht* version of Hanomag's commercial *Gigant* (Giant) tractor which was designed for train weights up to 20 tons. The vehicles are towing fuel for V-2 rockets. *(TM)*

The Type 94 was powered by either a diesel or petrol engine. In 1937, it was replaced by the improved Type 96, which featured improvements to the transmission and was fitted with a winch at the rear. The original Type 94 6x4 truck chassis was also used as a mount for a 20mm anti-aircraft gun intended to provide air defence for tank divisions.

The Japanese Imperial Army also used large numbers of full-tracked prime movers, rated at 3, 4, 5, 8 and 13 tons and intended for towing all types of artillery. Constructed at the Kokura or Sagami Arsenals, early models used petrol engines, but by around 1936/37 diesel engines had become standard equipment. Some 5,500 examples were constructed in total, most (1983) being of the Ro-Ke 6-ton type designed for towing either a 100mm cannon or 150mm howitzer.

Soviet Union

The Soviet Union used large numbers of fully-tracked prime movers for towing field guns and artillery, with light, medium and heavy types produced throughout the war. Most were bonneted vehicles, featuring an enclosed steel cab, with an open cargo box at the rear which could also be used for carrying personnel. Some were simply agricultural tractors which had been

pressed into military service, others were designed and built specifically for the Red Army.

The largest of these was the 22-ton Voroshilovets produced by Kharkov Locomotive Works and subsequently at the Stalingrad Tractor Works (STZ). Development had started in 1935, but the first production vehicles did not appear until 1939. The vehicle was fitted with scissor-type suspension with two bogies per side, each with four small road wheels. A 38,800cc V12 diesel engine, similar to that fitted in the T-34 medium tank, was used to power the vehicle.

More than 2,000 examples of the 14-ton Komintern were produced, also at the Kharkov Locomotive Works, between 1934 and 1941. This was designed to tow the 152mm howitzer.

Most numerous were the Stalinets S-60 and S-65, a medium agricultural tractor broadly modelled on the US-built Caterpillar Sixty which had been introduced in 1925; more than 100,000 examples of the two models were produced, a proportion of which were used by the Red Army. Most were equipped with a diesel engine, although a number of the SG-65 variant were fitted with a producer gas unit.

The smallest tractors were the 8-ton YaG-12, the STZ 3 and the 5-2TB. The YaG-12 was produced at the Yaroslavl Automobile Plant and

Above: Japanese Ikegai KO-HI Type 98 semi-track prime mover. Produced from 1937 as a tractor and self-propelled mount for anti-aircraft guns. *(AN)*

Right: The appalling conditions encountered during Soviet winters led to the Red Army's widespread use of full-tracked prime movers. Front three-quarter view of the KhPZ Komintern. The suspension was derived from that used on the T-12 tank and the tractor was capable of a maximum speed of almost 20mph (30km/h). *(PW)*

Right: *Voroshilovets* heavy prime mover. Initially constructed by Kharkov Locomotive Works in 1939, production was moved to Stalingrad (STZ) where the tractor continued to be produced until 1941, by which time 230 had been built. *(PW)*

Right: The YaG-12 light prime mover was introduced in 1943 and remained in production until 1945. Power was provided by a GM 4-71 two-stroke diesel. *(PW)*

Left: US-built Allis-Chalmers HD7W crawler tractor - or 'tractor, medium, M1' - being used by the Red Army to tow the 152mm M1937 howitzer in a 1945 victory parade. *(PW)*

Below: KhPZ Komintern medium prime mover. Some 2,000 of these tractors were constructed by Kharkov Locomotive Works between 1934 and 1941. The timber rear body provided accommodation for the gun crew; the cab was from the ZIS-5 truck. *(PW)*

Right: Morris-Commercial C8 4x4 designed as a Portee for the 2-pounder anti-tank gun. *(ST)*

was powered by a US-designed 4,655cc General Motors 4-71 two-stroke diesel engine. The vehicle was fitted with torsion-bar suspension and track system from the Soviet T-60 light tank. The YaG-13F variant used a Soviet-designed petrol engine. The STZ 3 and 5-2TB were both of forward-control design and were powered by a 7,460cc four-cylinder water-cooled petrol engine.

Intended as a fast towing vehicle for the 37mm light gun, the Komsomolets was an armoured vehicle derived from a Soviet light tank and powered by a GAZ-M petrol engine.

Right: Diamond T Model 981 (with the fairlead roller in the bumper) ballast tractor. More than 6,500 examples were built from 1941. Diesel-powered Diamond Ts remained in service with the British Army until the early 1970s. *(ST)*

Left: A 7 ¹/₂-ton Mack NO prime mover finished in post-war Glossy Deep Bronze Green. First built in 1940, the NO remained in production until 1945. The vehicle was intended for towing heavy artillery, particularly the US Army's 155mm 'Long Tom' howitzer. Many served with the British Army into the 1950s. *(ST)*

United States of America

US Army tractors fall into three clear groups – heavy wheeled tractors intended for tank transporting or towing heavy artillery, full-tracked so-called 'high speed' artillery tractors and full-tracked crawlers which could be used for towing artillery or engineers' plant.

The most impressive of all tank transporters is the mighty M25. This was made up of either a 6x6 soft-skinned Pacific TR1 M26 or armoured M26A1 tractor and a purpose-

Left: The Diamond T Model 980/981 was produced in both open and closed cab form and was initially intended for the British. It was adopted by the US Army as the M19 tank transporter initially classified as 'substitute standard', later downgraded to 'limited standard' when the M26 'Dragon Wagon' entered service. *(ST)*

Right: One of the strangest US vehicles of World War Two was the Walter ADUM, a 5-ton 4x4 tractor intended for towing the 155mm gun. Small numbers were built between 1940 and 1941. Note the contrast in scale to the Bantam Jeep prototype. *(TM)*

Above: Introduced in February 1944, the Albion CX22S heavy artillery tractor was developed from the company's 10-ton CX23N truck and was intended to supplement the Scammell R100 Pioneer. *(TM)*

designed 45-ton capacity Fruehauf M15 semi-trailer. The basic M26 could also be used for tank retrieval duties. Power was provided by a massive 17,862cc Hall-Scott six-cylinder water-cooled petrol engine driving the rear wheels via a Knuckey chain-driven bogie.

The Dart Truck Company of Kansas City, Missouri also produced the T3, a wheeled tractor capable of being used with the Fruehauf M15 semi-trailer.

Although it was rated as 'substitute standard', partly because of a non-standard diesel engine, the

US Army also used the Diamond T Model 980/981 which was being supplied to Britain and the other Allies. In fact, once the US entered the war, the US Army took the bulk of the approximately 6,500 produced between 1941 and 1945. Early production was fitted with a stylish 1930s-type cab, but from August 1943 this was replaced by a simple canvas-covered open cab with folding windscreen. The British also adapted the Diamond T for use with a 30-ton semi-trailer.

Wheeled artillery tractors were largely supplied by Mack, the company's 11,586cc petrol-engined NO and NQ models being rated at $7^1/_2$ tons and easily capable of hauling the US Army's massive 8in field gun or the 155mm howitzer. The Mack NM series, a 6 ton petrol-engined 6x6 cargo truck, could also be utilised as an artillery prime mover.

Small numbers of 8 ton prime movers were also supplied by International. Diamond T's cargo-bodied 4 ton 6x6 chassis was also used as an artillery tractor.

The Minneapolis-Moline GTX $7^1/_2$ ton 6x6 prime mover is interesting, although it appears not to have been used on active service, with all production vehicles somehow ending up in

Above: A Diamond T Model 980/981 with an oversized load. The standard 40/45-ton multi-wheeled tank transporter trailer has been cleverly adapted in the field to carry this landing craft. *(IWM)*

Brazil. Powered by a 9,911cc six-cylinder petrol engine, it was designed to haul the 90mm anti-aircraft gun. The design drew heavily on the company's expertise in producing heavy agricultural machinery.

Although it has not been included in the table, the short-wheelbase GMC 2¹/₂ ton 6x6 (CCKW-352) was occasionally pressed into service as an artillery tractor.

Diesel-powered crawler tractors were produced to similar designs, in the light, medium and heavy classes, by Allis-Chalmers, Caterpillar and International. Although intended for towing artillery as well as fulfilling various engineering duties, these tractors were often pressed into service as battlefield retrieval vehicles (if not transporters) for tanks and other disabled armoured vehicles.

The Cleveland Tractor Company (Cletrac) MG1 and MG2 were high-speed tractors designed for towing aircraft. The vehicles were fitted with a compressor mounted at the rear and driven by the main engine. A 100V, 3kW auxiliary generator was also carried.

Most interesting are, perhaps, the fully-tracked high-speed artillery tractors produced by Allis-Chalmers and International, rated at 13, 18 and 38 tons, and designated M5, M4 and M6, respectively. The bodies of these vehicles were designed to accommodate the gun crew and to provide stowage for standard ammunition boxes. The largest was the 38-ton M6, a monstrous machine capable of towing a 50,000lb (22,680kg) load, and powered by two 13,388cc Waukesha six-cylinder water-cooled petrol engines, each producing 190bhp. Typical artillery pieces which would have been towed by these tractors included the 3inch and 90mm anti-aircraft guns, 4.5inch and 155mm field guns, and 8inch and 240mm howitzers.

Also worthy of mention are the tracked over-snow machines produced by Allis-Chalmers and the Iron Fireman Company, intended for the rescue of downed aircraft crews. The half-tracked Allis-Chalmers M7 was powered by the 2,199cc Willys Go-Devil engine from the Jeep. To travel over deep snow, the front wheels could be replaced by skis. A special 1-ton trailer was designed for use with the vehicle. The full-tracked Iron Fireman T36 was powered by a 3,772cc Dodge six-cylinder petrol engine.

Above: The Mercedes-Benz DBs 7 of 1934 was the forerunner of the standardised SdKfz.8 12-ton half-track. The later DBs 10 variant was the most numerous of the series and was widely used as an artillery tractor and prime mover. (UB)

Right: The 18-ton SDKfz 9 - otherwise known as the FAMO F2 - was the largest of the German half-tracks, entering production in 1938. Power was provided by a standardised Maybach V12 petrol engine. (ST)

dit: ullstein - SV-Bilderdienst

Left: Aside from the *Kettenkrad* half-track motorcycle, the Demag D7 (SdKfz10) was the smallest of the German half-tracks being rated at 1 ton. It was used a prime mover for anti-tank artillery and as a self-propelled mount for anti-aircraft guns; there was also an armoured variant designated SdKfz250. *(UB)*

Below: The superbly restored SDKfz 9 from the Wheatcroft Collection. *(ST)*

Right: The Morris-Commercial CD/SW tractor coupled to one of its intended loads, the British 25-pounder field gun. The vehicle was subsequently used as a tractor for a Bofors anti-aircraft gun. *(PW)*

Right: The US-built 18-ton Mack EXBX tank carrier was originally ordered by the French as a fuel tanker. Following the fall of France in 1940, vehicles were diverted to the UK where they were adapted for tank transporting duties. *(IWM)*

Left: AEC Matador medium artillery tractor towing a 3.7inch anti-aircraft gun. *(TM)*

Below: Scammell R100 Pioneer heavy artillery tractor coupled to a British 7.2inch howitzer. The big steel body was designed to accommodate the gun crew as well as carrying stores and ammunition; a chain operated hoist and runway system was provided to assist handling heavy ammunition. *(PW)*

Right: Bedford MWG 15cwt truck being used as a Portee for the 2-pounder anti-tank gun. The aero screens and lack of doors indicate that this is an early production example. *(TM)*

Below: Column of Bedford MWG trucks equipped with anti-aircraft guns. *(TM)*

Left: Canadian Military Pattern (CMP) 15cwt 4x2 vehicle for mounting a 20mm anti-aircraft gun. *(PW)*

Left: Diamond T Model 980 tractor unit hauling a British Churchill tank on the standard 40-ton multi-axle trailer as manufactured by Cranes or Dyson. *(IWM)*

Left: A rare photograph of a Dart T13 tractor coupled to the M15 40-ton semi-trailer, the whole rig being described as the 'T3 truck-trailer, 40-ton, tank transporter'. The vehicle was built in 1942 by the Dart Truck Company of Kansas City as a possible contender for the heavy tank transporter contract which eventually was awarded to Pacific Car & Foundry. *(PW)*

Right: In the Western Desert, the combination of the steeply-raked trailer and the high-profile M3 Lee Grant tank mean that this Scammell Pioneer TRMU30/ TRCU30 is presenting an easy target to the enemy. *(IWM)*

Below: This rare Leyland is the second of two constructed as an experimental rigid-chassis tank transporter. It was based on a stretched Hippo chassis with a 10x4 drive-line. The vehicle would have been of little use for the heavier tanks which appeared in the later years of the war. The load is an early Crusader. *(TM)*

Top: Open-cabbed Diamond T with a captured German Jagdpanzer IV L70 with the longer 76mm gun. *(AN)*

Above: The Diamond T was also frequently coupled to the US-built 45-ton multi-wheeled trailer as typically produced by Rogers and others. *(TM)*

Left: The tow rope suggests that this Scammell Pioneer TRMU-30/TRCU-30 tractor and semi-trailer combination is bogged down. The load on the 30-ton trailer is a an infantry tank Mk II (Matilda). *(IWM)*

6 | Wreckers and Recovery Vehicles

The design of recovery vehicles changed little throughout the war, most vehicles consisting essentially of a heavy-duty truck chassis mounting a jibbed crane and a recovery winch.

The US standard design was the M1 heavy wrecker, which effectively dated from the mid-1930s, and the standard German wheeled recovery vehicle was similar. On the British side, although the Scammell SV/2S did not appear until the outbreak of war, and was mounted on a pre-war chassis with a fixed crane, the vehicle lacked the versatility of the US and German twin-boom designs.

Hydraulics had yet to have any influence on the design of lifting gear, and both the British and US vehicles initially employed manually-operated lifting jibs. The US Army's M1A1 of 1943 being the first to be fitted with a powered winch on the jib. As well as the crane and recovery winch, the typical vehicle was fitted with a specialised body which provided stowage for the tools and equipment likely to be required during recovery operations. This included some kind of earth anchor for use during winching operations.

Curiously, the German, Italian and Japanese Armies had very little in the way of specialised recovery equipment, apparently preferring instead to use heavy tractors in combination with low-loading trailers.

The Red Army had no domestic recovery vehicles, but was supplied with large numbers of American trucks under the Lend-Lease program.

Australia

Australia produced a number of 3-ton recovery vehicles using both domestic manufactured and imported chassis.

The earliest, dating from 1940, used a Marmon-Herrington all-wheel drive conversion of the Ford 11T chassis. The vehicle was of the typically-British gantry type, with a travelling pulley block for hoisting and an under-chassis recovery winch. Similar vehicles were constructed using the GM-Holden C60X chassis with the typical Canadian Military Pattern (CMP) cab, and generally badged Chevrolet. The Ford/Marmon-Herrington 296T chassis of 1942 was also used.

Above and left:
Constructed in almost identical form by US-based truck builders Kenworth and Ward LaFrance, the M1A1 heavy wrecker was standardised in 1943. The vehicle became the US Army's standard heavy recovery type into the early 1950s, replacing the early M1 models. The Gar Wood 5-ton swinging-boom crane was power operated. Production finished in 1945. *(ST)*

Above: The British Army-pattern 3-ton breakdown gantry body was fitted to Austin, Guy, Crossley (shown), Dodge and Leyland 6x4 chassis. A travelling pulley block was installed on the gantry which could be extended over the rear of the truck. A 5-ton capacity winch was fitted under the body. *(PW)*

Something of a hybrid was the Maple Leaf 1600 based recovery vehicle which used a 1940 Canadian GM (Chevrolet) truck chassis fitted with a GM-Holden steel cab, Harvey-Frost type tilting crane and locally-produced recovery body.

Canada

Canadian-produced recovery vehicles were generally of the 3-ton CMP pattern. Holmes or Gar Wood twin-boom, power-operated wrecking gear was mounted on both the Chevrolet long- and short-wheelbase C60S and C60L 4x4 chassis. More rarely, the same wrecking gear was fitted on the Chevrolet C60X 6x6 and Ford F60H 6x4, the latter with a curious lack of drive to the rear-most axle.

The Ford F60H was also used as the basis of a 3-ton gantry equipped vehicle, using British equipment with a maximum 2½ ton lift.

More unusual was the Ford EC098T assembled at the Ford factory in Dagenham, Essex. These vehicles mounted US-designed

Holmes Speed King twin-boom wrecking gear on a 1940-type Canadian Ford chassis/cab unit. Similar equipment was also mounted on the Chevrolet 15-43 chassis.

Germany

The largest German wheeled recovery vehicle was of similar design to the US Army's medium wrecker, and carried a manually-operated twin-boom crane in the style of the Holmes or Gar Wood equipment, mounted on the Büssing-NAG 4500A-1 and 4500S-1 heavy four-wheeled chassis. Similar equipment was also mounted on the MAN-designed leglELkw standardised 6x6 2½ ton chassis.

The mighty Famo F2/F3 18-ton half-track was also used as the basis for a recovery vehicle, mounting a choice of three cranes. Smallest of these was the SdKfz.9, using a recovery crane more usually fitted to a standardised heavy truck. There was also a manually-operated 6-ton August Bilstein revolving crane, in which condition the vehicle was designated

SdKfz.9/1, and a 10-ton fully-powered Bilstein petrol-electric crane, this variant being designated SdKfz.9/2.

Great Britain

The standard British heavy recovery vehicle - or 'breakdown' as it was described at the time - was the Scammell Pioneer, a heavy 6x4 chassis originally dating back to the early 1930s. In recovery vehicle form it had been introduced in 1939 as the SV/1T and SV/1S, using a collapsible A frame to support a horizontal jib. After just 43 examples had been constructed, this was superseded by the SV/2S, fitted with two-position sliding crane jib supplied by Herbert Morris. A total of 1,975 examples of the SV/2S were manufactured, with the last contract dated July 1945, but it was always in short supply and had to be supplemented by Lend-Lease vehicles from the US. On both models, a hand-operated worm-drive winch was provided for hoisting work. An 8-ton recovery winch was fitted between the chassis

rails. All Pioneers were fitted with a 8,369cc Gardner 6LW six-cylinder water-cooled diesel engine driving the rear wheels through a six-speed gearbox, and featured Scammell's extraordinary gear-driven walking-beam rear bogie and swing-axle front suspension.

On the lighter side, the Crossley 30/70 was a pre-war chassis fitted with a Harvey Frost 5-ton, fixed-jib crane; the same equipment was also mounted on the Crossley 4x4 forward-control chassis in 1940.

Also of pre-war design was the Morris-Commercial CDSW, a 30cwt 6x4 truck which had originally entered production in 1935. The 'light breakdown' variant dated from 1938 and was fitted with a fixed-jib crane carrying a hand-operated pulley block. The vehicle was equipped with a $4^{1}/_{2}$ ton under-floor recovery winch.

Introduced in 1944, the 6x4 Austin K6 was fitted with a $2^{1}/_{2}$ ton maximum capacity longitudinal gantry with a manually-operated travelling winch block; the front end of the gantry could be dropped to the floor to increase

Above: Improvised by a REME unit in Italy, here we see the complete body and jib equipment of a Scammell Pioneer SV/2S recovery vehicle fitted to a 6-ton Mack NM 6x6 chassis. *(PW)*

125

Above and left: The 4-ton 6x6 Diamond T Model 969 medium wrecker was equipped with the W45 twin-boom recovery gear supplied by Ernest Holmes of Chattanooga; each boom was rated at 5 tons but the two could be used together for a 10-ton lift. *(ST)*

Far left (both): The Model 969 was constructed only with a closed cab but the later Models 969A and 969B used both open and closed cabs. Total production of this chassis, which was also equipped for a variety of other roles, came to more than 31,000 units. *(RG/TM)*

Above: The Diamond T Model 969 medium wrecker was an extraordinarily handsome vehicle, particularly in its original closed-cab form. Many remained in service with European armies into the 1970s. *(RG/TM)*

Right: An M1A1 heavy wrecker in post-war US Army Air Force livery. The huge angled front bumper was reinforced for use as a pusher. *(PW)*

Above: The Gardner-powered Scammell Pioneer was used as the basis for two types of heavy recovery vehicle for the British Army. *(PW)*

Left: The original SV/1S used a folding jib, whilst on the more numerous SV/2S (above) the jib was of the sliding type. The lack of front-wheel drive was more than offset by the extraordinary axle articulation which gave the vehicle excellent off-road performance. *(TM)*

Above: Regardless of manufacturer, the M1A1 heavy wrecker was powered by a six-cylinder Continental 22R engine of 8,226cc producing close to 150bhp. *(RG/TM)*

Right: A 3-ton Austin K6/A 6x4 breakdown gantry vehicle, introduced in 1944. *(ST)*

Above: Scammell Pioneer SV/2S heavy recovery vehicle. Almost 2,000 were produced between 1939 and 1945. The last did not leave British Army service until the early 1980s. *(ST)*

Left: Morris-Commercial CDSW 30cwt 6x4 light recovery vehicle. *(ST)*

Above: Morris-Commercial CDSW light breakdown truck. The chassis entered production in 1935 and was also equipped for a variety of other roles.The jib carried a 1-ton manual hoist. A 4-ton winch was installed under the chassis. *(PW)*

Right: The Mack LMSW heavy recovery vehicle as supplied to the British Army. The steel body and recovery equipment, which was of the Scammell-type mould, consisted of an extensible jib and recovery winch. The equipment was supplied either by Gar Wood (model LMSW-23) or Mack (LMSW-39). A total of 374 were built between 1941 and 1942. *(IWM)*

the height of lift. A 5 ton winch was also fitted. Similar equipment was mounted on Ford, Guy, Crossley, Leyland and (American) Dodge chassis of varying ages, the latter being converted to 6x4 configuration by fitting a Thornton bogie.

Also worthy of mention is the fact that the British War Office almost took delivery of an air-portable twin-boom wrecker using the 6x6 Mack NM6 chassis... sadly, the contract was cancelled as the war ended before production commenced.

Italy

Derived from the Tipo 40 artillery tractor, and first appearing in 1941, the Breda 41 was the only purpose-designed recovery vehicle deployed by the Italian Army. With huge wheels, twinned at the rear, 8,850cc diesel engine and short wheelbase, the vehicle was typical of the manufacturer's military production. The Tipo 40 was equipped with independent front suspension, lockable differentials and hub-reduction gears. The fixed-jib crane was demountable and could be stowed on the sides of the vehicles body when not required.

Other medium and heavy truck chassis were also equipped for the recovery role, including the Ceirano 47CM.

Japan

Produced by the Kokura or Sogami State Arsenals, the Japanese Type 95 Ho-Fu full-tracked diesel-engined recovery vehicle appeared in 1941, but little else is known about the vehicle.

United States of America

Largest of all US recovery vehicles was the M1 heavy wrecker, a 6x6 design which dated back to the mid-1930s. Early examples were constructed by Corbitt and Marmon-

Below: Ward LaFrance 1000 Series 4 M1 heavy wrecker, dating from 1943; the Series 4 was the last of the line, and can be identified by the curved boom and pusher-type front bumper. The M1 was the first fitted with power-operated recovery equipment, and produced by Ward LaFrance in 1940. Similar versions were built by Kenworth. *(TM)*

Left: Using the chassis and running gear of the 18-ton FAMO F2 half-track (SdKfz9), the *Wehrmacht* specified the F3 heavy recovery vehicles primarily for tank recovery duties. Two types were built, one with a 6-ton manually-operated crane (SdKfz9/1), the other using a 10-ton petrol-electric powered crane (SdKfz9/2). *(UB)*

Above: Chevrolet Canadian Military Pattern (CMP) C60S recovery vehicle. This vehicle was constructed in two versions and is fitted with a 5/10-ton swinging-boom crane supplied by Gar Wood. *(TM)*

Herrington, but by 1940/41 production had settled on Kenworth and Ward LaFrance, the latter producing the majority of the 2,030 vehicles which had been delivered by the time the war ended. Powered by a 8,226cc Continental 22R six-cylinder water-cooled petrol engine, the vehicle featured a single Gar Wood Industries' manually-operated swinging-boom crane, rated at 5 tons, together with two winches mounted behind the cab.

In 1943, the M1 was revised and standardised as the M1A1, with a power-operated crane. The closed cabs of the early M1 machines were replaced by a typical open-cab design with crude, squared-off front mudguards. By this stage the differences between the products of the two manufacturers were very minor; the vehicle remained in production until 1945 by which time some 3,575 examples had been produced.

From 1941 the standard US Army medium wrecker was supplied by Diamond T using the short-wheelbase variant of the company's 4 ton 6x6 military chassis, powered by an 8,669cc Hercules RXC six-cylinder petrol engine. Although it was initially fitted with the company's stylish art-deco 'de-luxe' cab, by late 1942 it was fitted with a standard open cab. A flat, two-piece hinged windscreen, canvas top and small front-hinged doors were fitted. The wrecking gear, supplied by Ernest Holmes of Chattanooga, had two swivel booms, each with a 5 ton winch. The winches could be combined to give a total pull of 10 tons or used separately, one used to anchor the vehicle and the other to provide a 5-ton pull to the side. A third winch, rated at 7$\frac{1}{2}$ tons, was mounted behind the front bumper for self-recovery. The Diamond T remained in production throughout the war years, with 6,240 produced.

A similar medium wrecker, also using twin-boom Holmes wrecking gear, was supplied by the Available Truck Company of Chicago.

The 5-ton Mack 6x4 LMSW was produced in two basic recovery variants. The LMSW-23 and LMSW-39 were equipped with a similar manual-type jib to that used on the British

Left: Chevrolet Canadian Military Pattern (CMP) C60S recovery vehicle with the 5/10-ton Gar Wood swinging-boom crane in operation. *(TM)*

Below: A 7¹/₂-ton Federal 605 6x6 wrecker as used by the US Army Air Force. The vehicle was fitted with a Gar Wood 10-ton crane and an under-slung winch at the rear. The same equipment was also mounted on the Biederman chassis. *(303rdbg)*

Army's Scammell SV/2S; a total of 374 were supplied to the British Army in 1941/42. Slightly different were the 290 LMSW-53 and LMSW-57 wreckers destined for the Canadian Army; these were fitted with Gar Wood twin-boom wrecking equipment and different bodies.

Produced by Available Truck, Biederman, Corbitt, Federal, Reo and Sterling, the 7¹/₂-ton C-2 wrecker was a 6x6 design supplied to the US Air Force and US Navy for recovering crashed aircraft, and for general lifting and towing duties. Very similar in design, regardless of supplier, the vehicles were equipped with a 10-ton crane with a single, swinging boom; on later models the boom was designed to telescope. A winch was underslung at the rear and a 110V 3kW generator powered the cab-mounted searchlights. The Reo and Federal models were powered by a 14,011cc Hercules HXD six-cylinder petrol water-cooled engine; Biederman, Corbitt and Sterling machines used 12,766cc Waukesha six-cylinder petrol engines.

Smaller numbers of other recovery vehicles were also supplied by Autocar, Dodge, International, Oshkosh and GMC; the latter using a gantry type crane fitted to the standard 2¹/₂-ton 6x6 CCKW chassis. The smallest such vehicle was the 1¹/₂-ton Ford 09W/MH, a 4x4 conversion by Marmon-Herrington.

7 | Truck-mounted Cranes

Truck-mounted cranes did not start to appear in any quantity in military service until the early years of the war when, typically, they were employed for dock-side work, handling heavy gun barrels and other parts, lifting and loading ammunition into aircraft, and other general hoisting work.

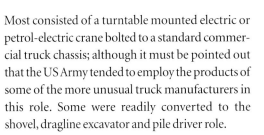

Most consisted of a turntable mounted electric or petrol-electric crane bolted to a standard commercial truck chassis; although it must be pointed out that the US Army tended to employ the products of some of the more unusual truck manufacturers in this role. Some were readily converted to the shovel, dragline excavator and pile driver role.

Australia

Where the US Air Force tended to use gantry style cranes for bomb loading, the Royal Australian Air Force employed a 3-ton rotating jib-type crane mounted on a locally-built International KS5 truck. Mechanical jacks were fitted ahead of the crane to stabilise the vehicle during lifting operations.

Canada

A simple derrick crane was mounted on the short-wheelbase Ford 3-ton F60S 4x4 Canadian Military Pattern (CMP) truck.

Germany

The German classification number for a crane was SdKfz96, and both 3-ton and 5-ton cranes were mounted on the standard diesel-engined heavy truck chassis, typically produced by Mercedes-Benz, Büssing-NAG and MAN.

The Famo 18-ton half-track (SdKfz9) was also used as a self-propelled mount for a manually-operated Bilstein 6-ton revolving crane, or a 10-ton fully-powered petrol-electric crane.

Great Britain

With a couple of exceptions, British truck-mounted cranes were rated at either 3 or 5 tons, and employed revolving electric or petrol-electric crane equipment supplied by H. J. Coles Limited of Derby, who provided more than 1,000 such cranes during World War Two. The DC generator which provided current for all of

Above: A 3-ton Austin K6 6x4 mounting a Coles EMA Mk VI electro-magnetic 3-ton crane. Rigid rear suspension was used to permit operation of the crane. *(PW)*

Left: A US Air Force Chevrolet G-7128 1½-ton 4x4 M6 bomb service truck. The vehicle was designed for loading, towing and unloading bomb-carrying trailers. *(PW)*

Above: A Leyland Retriever 3-ton 6x4 chassis fitted with a Coles 5-ton petrol-electric fully-rotating crane. The crew are using the jib as a walkway as they erect camouflage netting. *(IWM)*

the crane operations - hoisting, derricking and slewing - was generally driven by a separate petrol engine, either a Ford 10hp four cylinder unit on 3-ton cranes or a Ford V8 for 5-ton cranes. The trucks designed to carry these cranes were generally standard designs from Austin, AEC, Thornycroft, etc, modifications being confined to rigid beam rear suspension fitted in place of the more usual semi-elliptical springs.

On the Leyland Retriever and Thornycroft Amazon cranes, the main generator was driven directly from a power take-off on the vehicle gearbox.

The Thornycroft Amazon was produced as both long (WF-8) and short-wheelbase (WF) types. The vehicle was fitted with either a petrol or diesel engine. The most common crane fitted was a

Coles. Some Amazons were fitted with a Neales & Rapid unit.

Derrick cranes were also mounted on winch-equipped chassis supplied by Crossley, Guy and Leyland.

United States of America

Although the US Army employed a large number of cranes during World War Two, mounted onto an equally varied range of truck chassis, the only model that was standardised was the M2 truck-mounted crane. Mounted onto a chassis produced by Thew Shovel, the M2 was specifically designed to handle the heavy components of the 8in gun and the 240mm howitzer when changing from the travelling to firing position, and vice versa; the

Left: US Army Engineers begin the task of assembling a pontoon bridge across the River Rhine at Remagen. The vehicle is a Corbitt 50SD6 mounted with a Coles crane. *(USNa)*

Left: A Bay City crane mounted on a U8144T 6x6 chassis lifting the pilot section of a pontoon bridge for crossing the River Rhine at Remagen. *(USNa)*

crane was specifically used to remove the cradle recoil mechanism and the gun barrel from transport wagons and to assist in assembling the gun. The rotating crane unit, built by Moto-Crane, was powered by a 6,620cc Waukesha engine and, at 11ft radius, the capacity of the cable-operated 22ft boom was 40,000lb. The chassis was powered by a Hercules HXC engine, driving all six wheels through a four-speed gearbox, and was generally found towing an M16 trailer, which was used to carry a clamshell excavator bucket and 10 baulks of timber for use on soft or marshy ground.

US Air Force bomb service cranes were fitted with a gantry and a travelling pulley block and were designed for towing bomb trailers and for loading bombs onto aircraft. The smallest was the $1/2$-ton M1, which used a Ford-Marmon chassis; the M6

was fitted to a $1^1/_2$-ton Chevrolet 4x4 chassis; whilst the largest, the M27, employed the standard GMC $2^1/_2$-ton CCKW. There was also a low-profile $1^1/_2$-ton machine, which used the Ford GTBS and GTBC chassis, and was intended for use by the US Navy.

The Brockway, FWD, Ward LaFrance and White B666, and the Corbitt 50SD6, were heavy-duty 6x6 trucks designed to carry metal bridge treadway sections and were fitted with a derrick crane to assist in the erection of the bridge. A compressor was also carried to assist in inflating the bridge pontoons. Similar chassis, designated C666, from these same manufacturers, as well as the Coleman G55A, were fitted with a Quickway E55 4-8 ton rotating crane and were used by the US Corps of Engineers.

8 | Fire Appliances and Snow Clearers

Military fire appliances fall into two distinct type. Domestic-type escape and pump machines required for use around military bases and for dealing, for example, with brush fires on training grounds and in most cases these would take the form of a civilian appliance with a typical military paint finish.

More specialised are the so-called fire-crash-rescue trucks designed to deal with the particular conditions arising from aircraft accidents. For this purpose the vehicles were fitted with CO_2 gas or foam distribution equipment.

Snow-clearing machinery was used by the RAF and the US Air Force for keeping runways open during difficult winter conditions.

Germany

The standard classification codes for fire appliances in the German Army were as follows:

Kfz343   Medium truck, fire-fighting, water
Kfz344   Medium truck, fire-fighting,
         hose tender
Kfz345   Medium truck, fire engine
Kfz346   Medium truck, fire-fighting, hose

The typical mount was the standardised medium 4x2 chassis but there is very little information available as to which manufacturers actually built the vehicles. Turntable ladders were also mounted on the standardised 6x6 light chassis or the 4x2 heavy chassis.

The 1935 Magirus M206 is thought to have been the first specialised German-manufactured fire appliance.

Great Britain

The listed vehicles include those supplied to the Auxiliary Fire Service (AFS), and to the National Fire Service (NFS), which replaced the AFS in 1941. The AFS and NFS were responsible for fire-fighting duties throughout World War Two. Standard equipment included an auxiliary towing vehicle (ATV), heavy duty and extra-heavy duty pump units. Escape and turntable ladders and a mobile dam unit were also carried.

The ATV was designed to provide crew accommodation and shelter for protection

Above: Austin K2 auxiliary towing vehicle (ATV) of the National Fire Service. Large numbers of these vehicles were equipped as towing vehicles for mobile fire pumps. The steel body provided some shelter and accommodation for the crew. *(ST)*

Left: Crossley Q 30/100 HP 4x4 fire tender carrying water, foam compound, and two carbon-dioxide cylinders; a 100gallon/min (4,540 litre/min) rear-mounted high-pressure pump supplied foam to hand-held lances. *(TM)*

Above: Leyland Beaver equipped with a TSC/Merry-weather 100ft (30m) turntable ladder. *(PW)*

during fire-fighting operations. A small petrol-engined pump was towed by the vehicle. The heavy pump unit mounted a 700 gallon/min (3,200 litre/min) powered component on a medium lorry chassis, built by either Austin, Ford or Morris-Commercial. The 1,100 gallon/min (5,000 litre/min) extra-heavy pump was mounted on an Austin or Bedford chassis. The dam unit, generally mounted on an Austin chassis, provided a water supply for first-aid and fire-fighting where the mains supply was compromised.

The RAF employed CO_2 and foam-generating equipment on Austin, Ford and

Crossley chassis to deal with aircraft fires. The RAF was also equipped with US-built appliances.

United States of America

In the US, pump and escape units were mounted on a variety of chassis, including those from the specialised fire appliance manufacturers such as American, LaFrance, Peter Pirsch and Maxim Motors. Frequently the fire-fighting body and equipment was supplied by specialist manufacturers.

Standard military chassis also used in the fire tender role include 1½-ton Ford and Chevrolet vehicles and 2½-ton GMC and International vehicles, commonly fitted with Maxim equipment.

Worthy of special mention is the smallest such appliance, a three-wheeled Indian motorcycle combination mounting low-pressure CO_2 equipment. The largest was the 6-ton 6x6 Brockway or Ward LaFrance truck mounting high-pressure foam fog equipment for dealing with aircraft fires. Reo and Sterling also supplied heavy 6x6 chassis to the US Navy and US Air Force for aircraft fire-fighting, this time mounting Cardox low-pressure CO_2 equipment.

Snow-clearing was usually accomplished by using plough and rotary-dispersal equipment supplied by specialist manufacturers and mounted onto standard heavy-duty all-wheel-drive truck chassis. These included vehicles manufactured by FWD, Diamond T, Sterling, Oshkosh and Walter.

Above: A column of auxiliary towing vehicles on the way to an incident. Note the fire pump towed by the leading vehicle. *(PW)*

Left: Austin K6 4x2 mobile dam unit (MDU) incorporating a pump, two 500-gallon (2,275 litre) water tanks and shelter for the crew. The pump is mounted behind the cab. *(PW)*

Right: A decidedly pre-war RAF ambulance appears to the far left, possibly constructed on the Morris-Commercial D 6x4 chassis which was much favoured by the Air Ministry. Next to this is a Crossley 30/100HP 6x4 dual-purpose foam/water fire tender, one of 100 similar Auto Fire Protection bodied 'aerodrome fire tenders' supplied to the RAF during 1935/36. On the right is a foam-laying fire tender constructed on the 3-ton 6x4 Fordson E917T chassis, another type commonly used by the RAF and which, intriguingly carries a civilian registration number. *(RAFM)*

Right: Fordson WOT1 hose layer of the RAF Fire School. Dating from 1938, the 3-ton 6x4 WOT1 was used for a range of specialised applications by the RAF. *(RAFM)*

Right: Fordson WOT1 fire-crash tender equipped with rear-mounted pumping equipment and a combined tank for water and foam compound. Several similar appliances were constructed on this and other 6x4 chassis. *(RAFM)*

Left: Fordson BB 2-ton with a Unipower 6x4 conversion, equipped with water and foam compound tanks and with bottles of compressed gas. *(PW)*

Below: Standardised for use by the RAF, the Crossley Type Q was a 3-ton 4x4 chassis; some 11,000 were built. As well as being used as a fire tender (shown), it was also fitted for the cargo, MT breakdown, tractor and workshop roles. *(PW)*

Above: A Chevrolet G-4100/G-7100 series 1$\frac{1}{2}$-ton 4x2 truck equipped as a 300 gallon/min (1,362 litre/min) pumper. The fire equipment was supplied by Maxim, using an AM Barton or Darley front-mounted centrifugal pump. *(PW)*

Right: A National Fire Service (NFS) Ford 7V escape unit. *(PW)*

Above: A Kew (Britain)-built 3-ton Dodge 82 or 82A in RAF service equipped with a simple snow plough for keeping runways clear. *(PW)*

Left: The working end of a Roto Wing high-speed snow plough. This equipment was driven by two Waukesha engines and was typically mounted to a 4x4 heavy truck chassis. Used by the US Navy and US Army Air Forces and by the Royal Canadian Airforce for runway clearance. *(PW)*

9 | Amphibians

There are obvious military advantages to designing vehicles which can travel on roads and waterways with equal ease. The earliest reference to a military amphibian is from the Hydro Motor Car Company of Canton, Ohio which produced an amphibious car in 1918.

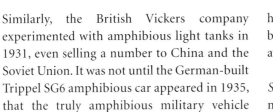

Similarly, the British Vickers company experimented with amphibious light tanks in 1931, even selling a number to China and the Soviet Union. It was not until the German-built Trippel SG6 amphibious car appeared in 1935, that the truly amphibious military vehicle became a practical proposition.

Although it would appear to be a simple enough task to install the automotive components of a car or truck into a sealed hull incorporating wheels, to allow the vehicle to run on road or tracks, and a propeller to provide propulsion in the water, most amphibious vehicles proved to be neither effective road vehicles nor satisfactory boats. It appears that the design parameters for the two modes of transport require the vehicle designer to make too many compromises, not least of which are the problems of providing sufficient airflow around the engine when the vehicle is operating in the water. And, on a practical level, obviously the axles or drive-shafts must pass through the hull. At the time, this placed a considerable burden on the materials and technologies available for sealing these apertures.

Nevertheless, the Porsche-designed VW *Schwimmwagen* and the US Army's DUKW are notable exceptions. The *Schwimmwagen* was as effective in deep mud or water as it was on the road. Without the DUKW it would have proved considerably more difficult for the Allies to deliver supplies from ships moored off the Normandy beaches in those few weeks following D-Day when no deep-water ports were available.

Other amphibians were also produced in Great Britain and Japan... but the DUKW and the VW *Schwimmwage*n remain the standard by which the type is judged.

Germany

The Trippel SG6 first appeared in 1935 and was produced by the Molsheim factory of Trippel Werke. Surprisingly sleek and attractive, it was

Above: A superbly restored *Schwimmwagen* fitted with original equipment. *(PR)*

Left: The VW Type 166 *Schwimmwagen* (Kfz1/20) was essentially an amphibious version of the Type 82 *Kübelwagen*. The rear-mounted propeller was carried on a hinged mount which swung down to engage with a dog clutch on the crankshaft. This meant there was no reverse gear - hence the paddles always carried. Some 14,000 examples were produced between 1942 and 1944. *(UB)*

Above: VW *Schwimmwagen* struggling through the snows of the Russian winter. Unlike the *Kübelwagen* cousin, the vehicle was equipped with all-wheel drive, and self-locking differentials, which made it a formidable performer in mud and snow. *(UB)*

initially offered to civilians as a four-seater dual-purpose vehicle, equally at home on road or water. Early examples were powered by a 2,000cc Adler four-cylinder petrol engine and fitted with all-round independent suspension. The propeller was housed inside the bodywork and could be raised or lowered as required.

The first military version, dating from 1938, was the all-wheel-drive SG6/38, an ugly, bathtub shaped vehicle with a widened two-door body, presumably to accommodate four well-equipped soldiers. By now it was powered by a 2,473cc Opel six-cylinder petrol engine driving through a five-speed gearbox. Most numerous was the SG6/41, which appeared in 1941 and featured a redesigned hull without doors. Approximately 1,000 examples were constructed. The SG7, from 1943, was powered by a Tatra V8 petrol engine. The E3 armoured version was produced in 1944.

Better known than the Trippel is the Volkswagen Type 166 K2s – the *Schwimmwagen*. Initially designated the Porsche 128, the machine appeared in 1940 as a

prototype with some 150 examples produced. The vehicle was effectively a four-wheel-drive amphibious version of the VW *Kübelwagen* with which it shared many automotive components, including the engine and torsion-bar suspension. The three-bladed propeller was mounted on a hinged bracket at the rear and could be swung down to engage in a dog clutch on the rear of the crankshaft. Top speed in water was 6mph (9.7km/h). Early versions featured a five-speed gearbox but this was later replaced by a four-speed unit; the differentials were self-locking which gave the vehicle formidable off-road performance. Because of the way the propeller was driven, the vehicle could not be reversed when afloat. A total of 14,265 were produced between 1942 and 1944.

The L-W-S (*land-wasser-schlepper* - land-water-tractor) was designed in the mid-1930s by Rheinmetall-Borsig and built by Alkett of Spandau, Sachsenberg of Dessau and Hattenwerke of Southhofen. The tractor was powered by a 10,838cc Maybach V12 300hp petrol engine mounted amidships. This drove

two propellers, each fitted with an in-line rudder. The vehicle did not enter service until 1940 and was intended as a prime mover on land and a tug on inland water; some were also used in pairs as ferries with a deck connecting the two hulls. It is thought that 21 constructed and, unlike most amphibians, performance in water was considerably better than the vehicle's performance on dry land.

Great Britain

Although Britain received large numbers of US-built DUKWs under the Lend-Lease program, there was also a British-designed, albeit considerably less-successful, amphibious truck.

The Terrapin Mk I was designed and built as a prototype by Thornycroft. Later some 500

Above: Britain's attempt at building a domestic rival to the DUKW was the eight-wheeled skid-steered Morris-Commercial Terrapin of which 500 examples were built. Designed by Thornycroft, the vehicle was powered by two Ford V8 petrol engines, each driving the four wheels along one side of the vehicle. The lack of suspension made it difficult to drive on the road. *(TM)*

Left: The 5-ton prototype for the Mk II version. *(PW)*

Right: DUKW crew training from a holiday beach in the USA. *(PW)*

Below: The US-built DUKW was designed by the naval architects Sparkman & Stephens who had been responsible for the GPA amphibious Jeep. The DUKW appeared in 1941 and, despite an uncertain beginning, was standardised for production in 1942. Using mechanical components from the 2$\frac{1}{2}$-ton GMC 6x6, the DUKW was probably the most successful amphibian of the war. More than 21,000 built. Late examples had a central tyre inflation system (CTIS) which allowed the driver to raise or lower tyre pressures to suit landing conditions. *(ST)*

Left: For the raid on Pointe du Hoc as part of the D-Day landings, 6 June 1944, four DUKW vehicles were fitted with a 82ft (25m) London Fire Brigade extending ladder mounted with two aircraft-type .303 Lewis machine guns. *(PR)*

examples were produced by Morris-Commercial between 1943 and 1944. Two 7,242cc Ford V8 water-cooled petrol engines, each drove the four wheels on one side of the vehicle via a three-speed gearbox. The vehicle had a 4-ton cargo capacity, which was a considerable improvement on the 2^1/$_2$ tons of the DUKW. Sadly, the lack of suspension combined with the wheel-braking steering system made the Terrapin something of a handful on the road. A number were used as an emergency flood barrier in East Anglia during 1953 and presumably still remain below the North Sea.

In 1945, Thornycroft produced five examples of the improved Mk II, which offered a 5-ton cargo capacity in an improved hull with a forward-positioned enclosed cab. The end of the war brought the project to a premature end.

Japan

Dating from November 1943, the Toyota KCY was a four-wheeled amphibian with a large steel hull to which was fitted external axles and suspension components. The vehicle was fitted with the 3,389cc six-cylinder petrol engine and transmission of the contemporary Toyota KC truck. Drive was to all four wheels via a four-speed gearbox and two-speed transfer case, or to the propeller via a power take-off point. Only 198 examples were produced during a 10-month production run.

United States of America

One of the most interesting vehicles produced by the US during the war was the 2^1/$_2$-ton GMC DUKW (D: 1942 design; U: amphibian; K: all-

Below: Two early
type DUKW's -
identifiable by the
vertical windscreen -
being for ferrying
trials. *(IWM)*

Right: Two DUKWs ferry a 2¹/₂-ton GMC 6x6 truck ashore. The DUKW was sea-going and could manage 6mph (10km/h) in the water. *(IWM)*

Below: A 2¹/₂-ton GMC truck being loaded on to the platform between the two DUKWs. The truck is an experimental load to test stability. *(IWM)*

Above: A special amphibious trailer was designed for use with the DUKW. *(IWM)*

wheel drive; W: tandem rear drive). The prototype, effectively an amphibious version of the GMC-designed AFKW forward-control truck, was developed in less than 40 days during Spring 1942 by Palmer C. Putman of the National Defense Research Committee and Roderick Stephens, Jr of the naval architects Sparkman & Stephens. When production started later that year the automotive components of the more-numerous CCKW were used.

The engine, transmission and most of the steering gear were installed inside the steel hull, with drive-shafts, springs, and axles outside. Steering was by the front wheels on the road and by a combination of the front wheels and a rear-mounted rudder when in the water. A large pusher propeller in a tunnel at the rear gave a maximum speed in the water of around 6mph (9.7km/h). Three bilge pumps were installed, and late models had a central tyre inflation system. A 10,000 lb-capacity Gar Wood winch was installed at the rear of the vehicle.

A total of 21,147 were produced between 1942 and 1945 and the type remained in service with the US Army until 1958. Surplus US Army DUKWs also served for many years with the British, French, Belgian, Italian Armies and with the *Bundesmarine* (German Navy).

Another vehicle also designed by Sparkman & Stephens was the Ford GPA, an amphibious version of the ubiquitous Jeep. The design was first built as a prototype by Marmon-Herrington in 1941 before the project was taken over by the Ford Motor Company. In production form the GPA had a small, boat-like hull on an extended version of the Ford GPW chassis. The vehicle was powered by the standard 2,199cc Willys 'Go Devil' four-cylinder petrol engine, driving either the wheels or a rear-mounted propeller via the standard three-speed gearbox and two-speed transfer case. The hull provided accommodation for four, and there was a 3,500lb-capacity capstan winch installed on the front. Production began in 1942 and 12,778 examples had been delivered before

Above: Captured *Schwimmwagen* which has been adopted by a US unit; note the high-flotation 200-12 tyres. *(PW)*

Left: Like the DUKW, the *Schwimmwagen* could manage 6mph (10km/h) in the water. *(JSS)*

Above: The
Sparkman &
Stephens designed
GPA was the US
equivalent of the
Schwimmwagen.
Originally prototyped
by Marmon-
Herrington, with
series production
by Ford, the vehicle
used Jeep
mechanical
components and
an extended Jeep
chassis. A total of
12,778 units were
built between 1942
and 1943. *(PW)*

production was cancelled in 1943. Although the vehicle performed well the GPA was not to be as useful as had been initially thought.

The curiously-named Aqua-Cheetah was the work of Roger W. Hofheins, a US engineer who was president of the Amphibian Car Corporation of Buffalo, New York. In mid-1941 he offered a prototype of a Ford V8-powered amphibious ¹/₂-ton vehicle to the US Army for trials. The engine was mid-mounted and drove either a single propeller at the rear, or all four wheels through trailing-arm chain cases. All-round independent coil-spring suspension was fitted.

Following trials, the original design, designated XAC-1, was revised using a 3,772cc six-cylinder petrol engine, gearbox and differentials of the ¹/₂-ton Dodge 4x4, the engine now mounted in the rear and coupled to a chain-driven transfer case. The relocation of the engine to the rear allowed more conventional seating for seven, a three-man bench at the front and a four-man bench at the rear. In an emergency, it was said that the vehicle could accommodate up to 12 men on the road and 21 on the water. Top speed on water was 6.5mph (10.5kph). A single example was supplied for trials in May 1942 and this

was followed by a contract for 14 vehicles. By mid-1942, the ³/₄-ton Dodge had been replaced by the ¹/₂-ton design and the Aqua-Cheetah XAC-3 was produced using this engine and running gear and, subsequently, 11 of the existing XAC-2 variants were converted to XAC-3 specification. In late 1942, the US Ordnance Corps cancelled all outstanding production of the Aqua-Cheetah. No further vehicles were produced.

The M28 Studebaker Weasel was introduced in 1942, and was a fully-tracked cargo carrier originally designed for over-snow operation. In revised M29 form the vehicle had a box-like steel hull with a 2,786cc Studebaker Champion six-cylinder water-cooled petrol engine installed alongside the driver. The engine drove jointed steel tracks via a three-speed gearbox and two-speed transfer case. Steering was via levers acting on a controlled differential. The shape of the hull meant that the basic vehicle could float making the vehicle an ideal subject for conversion to an amphibian.

In 1943, the M29C fully-amphibious variant appeared, sometimes known as the Water Weasel. Buoyancy was improved by the addition of watertight steel compartments at

the front and rear of the hull, while two propellers and a new type of 20in (51cm) wide tracks provided propulsion in the water. Steering on water was by two rudders. Track skirts, a surf guard and a deck-mounted capstan winch were fitted on the vehicle.

Maximum speed on the road was 45mph (72km/h); on the water, 3.5mph (5.6km/h).

The total number built, during a two-year production run was 10,647. The vehicle was so reliable that a number were still in service up until the 1960s.

Above and left:
The US-built XAC-2 Aqua Cheetah was a ¹/₂-ton 4x4 amphibian powered by a rear-mounted Dodge engine driving the wheels via chains, and with a propeller drive from the gearbox. Only 12 examples were built by the Amphibious Car Corporation in 1942, most of which were rebuilt in upgraded XAC-3 form in 1943. One example was apparently sent to the UK. The hull provided seating for six and speed in the water was a little more than 6mph (10km/h). *(PW)*

10 | Ambulances and Medical Vehicles

Regardless of country of origin, the role of an ambulance is to move the sick or wounded to a place of safety such as a casualty clearing station, field hospital or civilian hospital.

Any distinction between different types of ambulance should firstly divide the vehicles into front-line ambulances, often with all-wheel drive, and those which have no military requirements, for example the American 'metropolitan'-type ambulances which were intended entirely for use on hard-surfaced roads. It would be fair to say that the basic ambulance requirement had changed little since World War One, albeit vehicles had become more reliable and comfortable. According to the size of the vehicle's body, an ambulance might have included accommodation for two or more stretchers, or four or more seated casualties, often with additional space for a medical attendant. Some vehicles, at least, also included a water tank, internal heater and stowage for blankets along with medical supplies.

It is also worth noting that buses were also pressed into service as makeshift ambulances; with the seats removed and double doors fitted at the rear, a bus body was capable of accommodating a significant number of stretchers. All of the major combatants also operated armoured ambulances, using standard wheeled or half-track armoured vehicle chassis.

Other vehicles listed here include mobile surgical units, dental surgeries, X-Ray facilities and medical laboratories.

Australia

Light ambulances produced for the Australian Army included an all-steel four-stretcher body mounted on a GM-Holden 1500 Series 3-ton chassis, also the so-named 'Indian Army' type, which was a World War One-pattern body mounted on a domestic 30cwt Chevrolet or Ford 4x2 chassis. Similar bodies were also mounted on Dodge and GMC chassis. There was also a domestic four-stretcher composite-type body mounted on the short-wheelbase 4x4 C60S Canadian Military Pattern (CMP) chassis.

Also worthy of mention is the Chevrolet 1541 30cwt truck, which was fitted with a

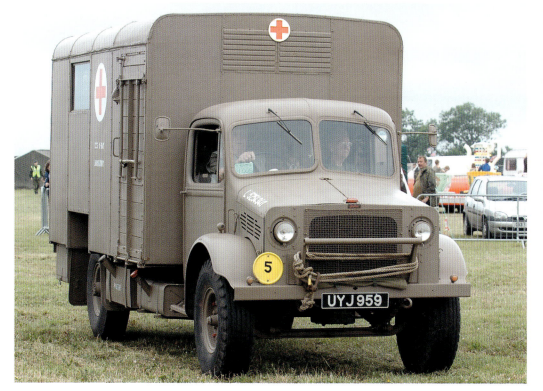

Above: The 4x2 Austin K2/Y was the British Army's standard heavy ambulance. The four-stretcher canvas-covered body was produced by Mann Egerton. *(ST)*

Left: The Bedford OY was introduced in 1939; the OYC variant was equipped as a mobile X-ray laboratory for use at casualty clearing stations (CCS). *(ST)*

Right: The Austin K2 was also supplied to other of the Allied nations. This example has been donated to the city of Stalingrad by the people of the British town of Scarborough. *(PW)*

Right: The Austin K2 was also supplied to other of the Allied nations. This example has been donated to the city of Stalingrad by the people of the British town of Scarborough. *(PW)*

Right: The British 8cwt Humber FWD chassis was used as a light ambulance with the advantage of all-wheel drive, The four-stretcher body was constrcted by Thrupp & Maberly. *(RAFM)*

refrigerated body unit for the transportation of blood plasma.

The Royal Australian Medical Corps (RAMC) also developed a Jeep-based ambulance suitable for emergency evacuation.

Canada

The 3-ton Ford C60 CMP chassis was used as the basis of a standard field ambulance for the Royal Canadian Army Medical Corps (RCAMC) field ambulance units and motor ambulance companies. The vehicle was used to transport wounded personnel between advanced dressing stations, field dressing stations, casualty clearing stations and hospitals. The 10ft (3.05m) long body, with interior heating, was designed to accommodate two stretcher and four seated casualties. The same chassis, this time supplied by Chevrolet, was also fitted-out as a dental surgery.

Chevrolet also supplied the 3-ton CMP chassis for use as a 'medical truck'; with a standard all-steel GS body equipped with two

Left: The steel-bodied Dodge WC54 (nicely contrasted here with the British Austin K2) was the US Army's standard ambulance during the war. The photograph was taken at Thorpe Abbotts airfield, home of the 303rd bomber group, part of the 8th US Air Force. On the skyline are dispersed B-17 'Flying Fortress' bombers. *(303rdbg)*

spring-supported stretchers and a bench for four seated casualties. The vehicle was intended for use as a regimental aid post or small field dressing station in forward areas.

Other 'medical' roles for CMP vehicles included the 3-ton Chevrolet C60H 6x6 chassis mounted with a laboratory body equipped for testing food, water, air samples and for general pathology work. An X-ray laboratory body was mounted on the Ford F60H variant.

Germany

The standard German Army ambulance (*Kranken-kraftwagen* [Krkw] or *Sanitätskraftwagen* [Sanka]) was identified as Kfz31. This body was fitted on a number of light truck chassis including the Steyr 640/643, Mercedes-Benz L1100 and L1500, Opel Blitz (4x2 and 4x4) and the Horch 40. It was also used on the Phänomen Granit 25H and 1500A, both on a four-wheel-drive chassis. Typically, the body included accommodation for four stretchers or eight seated casualties.

Mobile operating theatres were also fitted on a number of medium truck chassis, including Ford (Taunus), MAN and Opel and possibly others.

After the occupation of France in 1940, Peugeot also produced ambulances for the *Wehrmacht*. A number of ambulances captured on the Eastern and Western Fronts were utilised by German forces.

Great Britain

At the outbreak of war, the British Army had just 1,700 ambulances, many of which were commandeered civilian types. The standard heavy ambulance of the time was the Morris-Commercial CS11 fitted with a fabric-type body built by coachbuilders Mann Egerton. Similar four-stretcher bodywork was also mounted on the same manufacturer's CDF 6x4 chassis. Smaller ambulances from the 1930s included a four-stretcher body on a Morris light commercial vehicle chassis. These were quickly supplemented by a four-stretcher all-wheel-drive ambulance bodied by Thrupp & Maberly on the 8cwt Humber FWD chassis.

By 1940 both of these had been superseded by the 2-ton Austin K2Y, again using an in the main fabric body constructed by coachbuilders Mann Egerton and designed to accommodate four stretcher or 10 seated casualties. Over 13,000 of these vehicles were manufactured and many were supplied to other nations, including France, the Soviet Union and the US.

Similar bodied vehicles were constructed in 1939/40 on the 2-ton Bedford ML chassis.

In 1939 a number of London Transport Green Line service single-deck AEC coaches had been pressed into service as six-stretcher ambulances to deal with multiple casualties resulting from bombing raids on London by the

Above and right:
Designated Kfz31, many 4x2 light truck chassis were equipped as *Sanitätskraftwagen* (ambulances) for the *Wehrmacht*. The Mercedes-Benz L1000 and LE1100 chassis were frequently used, as well as the L1500 shown. *(PR)*

Luftwaffe. By 1940 it was obvious that these vehicles were not required; some were fitted out as dental surgeries and others were converted for use as Clubmobiles by the US Red Cross.

The RAF continued to use the Albion AM463 ambulance which dated back to the mid-1930s, together with a light four-stretcher design constructed on the Standard 14 chassis. These were supplemented by the ambulance version of the Fordson WOT1.

The British Carter stretcher equipment was also adapted for mounting on the Jeep to provide a lightweight field expedient ambulance.

The total number of ambulances in service with the British Army by VE Day was 15,309 which also included types of US and Canadian origin.

Italy

The Fiat 618M and SPA 38R 4x2 truck chassis were used to mount a standard ambulance body; the latter providing a larger capacity.

Japan

Imperial Army ambulance bodies were typically mounted on Isuzu Type 94 truck chassis, either the 4x2 or 6x4 Type 94A

petrol-engined variant, or the Type 94B diesel-engined 6x4 version.

Soviet Union

The Red Army used large numbers of British Austin K2Y and US-built Dodge ambulances, supplied under the Lend-Lease Program.

Domestic ambulances were built on GAZ-05-193, Zis-16C and GAZ-55 chassis; the former was a more softly-sprung and otherwise modified version of the 6x4 GAZ-AAA civilian

truck chassis. The latter was similarly derived from the 4x2 GAZ-AA.

The GAZ-05-293 provided seated accommodation for nine casualties, whilst the GAZ-55 had space for four stretcher cases together with two seated. Both vehicles were powered by the same type 3,285cc four-cylinder water cooled pertol engine.

United States of America

The US Army used civilian 'metropolitan'-type ambulances for delivering patients from bases to hospitals and for general behind-the-lines use. Typically, such vehicles had a four-stretcher all-steel body constructed by companies such as Henney, Hess & Eisenhart and Superior. The bodies were mounted on the lengthened chassis of a large motorcar, for example a Cadillac, Packard or LaSalle.

Although Chevrolet and Ford chassis dating from 1939/42 were used as the basis of a 4x2 field ambulance. The standard field ambulance for all of World War Two was the Dodge WC Series, an all-wheel-drive chassis first produced as a $^{1}/_{2}$-ton vehicle in 1940 but quickly standardised as the $^{3}/_{4}$-ton WC54 the following year. The body, constructed by Wayne, was an all-steel panel-van

design providing accommodation for four stretcher or seven seated casualties. Some 26,000 were produced between 1942 and 1944, with a further 3,500 of the WC64 'knock-down' (KD) design on the same chassis in 1945. The KD body, which provided the same patient accommodation, could be folded down for ease of transport by air.

Also worthy of mention are the 28-foot (8.5m) long Ford-powered 'mobile army surgical hospital' (MASH) vehicles constructed on coach chassis supplied by Linn Coach & Truck Company of Oneonta, New York in 1940. Four or five such vehicles could be linked together to form a MASH unit. A total of 25 were supplied between 1940 and 1945, when the standardised M423 design was introduced.

Surgical and dental facilities were commonly installed on the standard $2^{1}/_{2}$-ton GMC long-wheelbase 6x6 chassis.

Jeeps were also adapted to provide an all-wheel-drive field ambulance, which could carry one or two stretcher cases on an improvised framework, either mounted above the windscreen, across the bonnet, or across the rear compartment. Whilst the Jeep may not have been comfortable, the vehicle was at least capable of crossing most types of difficult terrain and were thus ideal for the emergency 'medevac' role.

Utility Vehicles

Make	Model	Description	Date	Engine: capacity	cylinders*
Australia					
Chevrolet	1216	Van, (pick-up), 12cwt, GS, 4x2	1942	3,548cc	6
	C15	Truck, utility, six seat, 4x2	1942	3,548cc	6
Ford	01Y	Van, (pick-up), 1 ton, GS, 4x2	1940	3,622cc	V8
	F15A	Truck, utility, six seater, 4x4	1942	3,548cc	6
International	K3	Van, (pick-up), 1 ton, GS, 4x2	1940	3,507cc	6
Plymouth	P11	Van, (pick-up), 12cwt, GS, 4x2	1941	3,294cc	6
Canada					
Chevrolet	C8A	Truck, heavy utility, cipher office, 4x4	1942	3,548cc	6
	C8A	Truck, heavy utility, computor, 4x4	1942	3,548cc	6
	C8A	Truck, heavy utility, machinery, 4x4	1942	3,548cc	6
	C8A	Truck, heavy utility, personnel, 4x4	1942	3,548cc	6
	C8A	Truck, heavy utility, wireless, 4x4	1942	3,548cc	6
Dodge	T116	Panel van, 1 ton, 4x2	1941	3,540cc	6
Ford	C11ADF	Station wagon/heavy utility, 4x2	1941	3,917cc	V8
	C15	Truck, six seater, utility	1942	3,548cc	6
	C21AS	Station wagon/ heavy utility, 4x2	1942	3,917cc	V8
	CO11DF-F8	Truck, heavy utility	1941	3,917cc	V8
Germany					
Adler	3GD	Car, medium, 4x2, Kfz12	1938	2,916cc	6
	HK300/A3F	Semi-track, light, command	1940	2,800cc	4
Ford	s.E.Pkw	Car, heavy, 4x4; Kfz21, Kfz70	1935	3,621cc	V8
	V8-48 Spezial	Car, heavy, 4x2; Kfz15	1938	3,621cc	V8
Hanomag	4/23	Car, light, 4x2	1932	1,097cc	4
	E.Pkw	Car, light, 4x4; Kfz4	1937	1,991cc	4
	Garant	Car, light, 4x2; Kfz2	1935	1,097cc	4
Horch	Type 40/901	Car, medium, 4x4; Kfz21	1937	3,517cc	V8
	Type 40	Car, medium, 4x4; Kfz15, Kfz21	1942	3,823cc	V8
	830R	Car, medium, 4x2; Kfz11, Kfz15, Kfz17	1934	3,250cc	V8
	m.E.Pkw	Car, medium, 4x4; Kfz12, Kfz15, Kfz17	1937	3,546cc	V8
	m.E.Pkw	Car, medium, 4x4; Kfz16, Kfz16/2	1937	3,823cc	V8
	1A, 1B	Car, heavy, 4x4; Kfz69	1937	3,823cc	V8
	40; s.E.Pkw	Car, heavy, 4x4; Kfz21, Kfz70	1935	3,823cc	V8
	850	Car, heavy, limousine, 4x2	1941	3,823cc	V8
	108 Type II	Van, 4x4; Kfz70	1937	3,823cc	V8
Krupp	L2H143	Car, heavy, convertible, 6x4	1940	3,500cc	4
Mercedes-Benz	170VK	Car, light, 4x2; Kfz2, Kfz2/40, Kfz3	1931	1,697cc	4
	G5/W152	Car, light, 4x4	1937	2,006cc	4
	170VL/W139	Car, medium, 4x4	1936	1,697cc	4
	200	Car, medium, 4x4	1932	2,000cc	6
	230	Car, medium, 4x2; Kfz12	1938	3,208cc	6
	320	Car, medium, 4x2; Kfz15	1937	3,208cc	6
	320WK	Car, medium, 4x2; Kfz12	1937	3,208cc	6
	320	Car, heavy, convertible, 4x2	1937	3,208cc	6
	L1500A	Car, heavy, 4x4; Kfz16	1941	2,594cc	6

* V = cylinders in Vee formation; H = flat or horizontally-opposed configuration.

Left: Troops from the Royal Engineers prepare to erect a temporary bridge over a river in Italy. Senior officers have arrived on the scene in British Army Jeeps. *(IWM)*

Make	Model	Description	Date	Engine: capacity	cylinders*
Mercedes-Benz	G4/W31	Car, heavy, six seater, 6x4	1934	5,018cc	8
(cont)	G4/W31	Car, heavy, six seater, 6x4	1937	5,252cc	8
	G4/W31	Car, heavy, six seater, 6x4	1938	5,401cc	8
	G4/W131	Car, heavy, six seater, 6x6	1937	5,252cc	8
	L1500A/L301	Car, heavy, personnel, 4x4; Kfz15, Kfz70	1938	3,208cc	6
Opel	P4	Car, light, 4x2; Kfz1	1937	1,074cc	4
	m.E.Pkw	Car, medium, 4x4; Kfz15, Kfz17	1942	3,517cc	6
	Super 6	Car, medium, 4x2; Kfz12	1938	2,473cc	6
Phänomen	Granit 1500A	Car, heavy, personnel, 4x4	1940	2,678cc	4
Skoda	Popular 1100	Car, light, 4x2; Kfz1 (Czech)	1939	1,100cc	4
	Superb 3000	Car, heavy, command; Kfz21 (Czech)	1942	3,140cc	6
	Superb 3000	Car, medium; Kfz15 (Czech)	1942	3,140cc	6
	Superb 903	Car, medium, 6x4 (Czech)	1942	3,140cc	6
Steyr-Puch	250	Car, medium, personnel, 4x2 (Austrian)	1939	1,200cc	4
	640	Car, heavy, command, 6x4 (Austrian)	1937	2,260cc	6
	1500	Car, heavy, command, 4x4; Kfz21 (Austrian)	1941	3,517cc	V8
	1500	Car, heavy, personnel, 4x4; Kfz21 (Austrian)	1941	3,517cc	V8
Stoewer	40	Car, light, 4x4; Kfz2, Kfz2/40, Kfz3, Kfz4	1940	1,997cc	4
	M12	Car, medium, 4x2; Kfz15	1935	3,000cc	V8
	R200 Spezial	Car, light, 4x4; Kfz1, Kfz2, Kfz2/40, Kfz3	1936	1,997cc	4
Tatra	T57K	Car, light, 4x2; Kfz1 (Czech)	1941	1,256cc	H4
	T87	Car, medium, 4x2 (Czech)	1938	2,960cc	V8
	V799	Car, medium, 4x2 (Czech)	1938	2,191cc	4
	T809	Car, medium, command, 4x4 (Czech)	1942	2,473cc	4
	T93	Car, heavy, convertible, 6x4 (Czech)	1937	3,980cc	V8
Tempo	G1200	Car, light, 4x4	1936	1,196cc	2x 2

* V = cylinders in Vee formation; H = flat or horizontally-opposed configuration.

Make	Model	Description	Date	Engine: capacity	cylinders*
Volkswagen	Type 82	Car, light, 4x2; Kfz1	1942	985cc	H4
	Type 82	Car, light, 4x2; Kfz1	1943	1,131cc	H4
Wanderer	m.E.Pkw	Car, medium, 4x4; Kfz15, Kfz17	1942	3,517cc	6
	W11	Car, medium, 4x2; Kfz11, Kfz12	1933	2,651cc	6
	W11	Car, medium, 4x2; Kfz11, Kfz12	1937	2,970cc	6
	W23S	Car, medium, 4x2; Kfz12	1937	2,651cc	6

Great Britain

Make	Model	Description	Date	Engine: capacity	cylinders*
Austin	10 Series G/YG	Car, light utility, 4x2	1939	1,230cc	4
Bedford	JCV Utilecon	Van, 10-12cwt, light utility, 4x2	1939	1,442cc	4
	BYC	Van, 12 cwt, utility van	1938	2,393cc	6
Ford	E83W Utilecon	Van, light utility, 4x2	1940	1,172cc	4
	WOA2	Car, heavy utility, 4x2	1941	3,621cc	V8
Hillman	10	Car, light utility, 4x2	1940	1,180cc	4
	10	Van, ladder, 4x2	1940	1,180cc	4
Humber	FWD	Car, heavy utility, 4x4	1940	4,086cc	6
	Snipe	Car, heavy utility, 4x2	1939	4,086cc	6
Morris	10 Series M	Car, light utility, 4x2	1939	1,140cc	4
Standard	12	Car, light utility, 4x2	1940	1,609cc	4
	12	Car, estate, (van), 4x2	1940	1,609cc	4

Italy

Make	Model	Description	Date	Engine: capacity	cylinders*
Fiat	508C 'Mil'	Truck, 350kg, light, 4x2	1939	1,089cc	4

Japan

Make	Model	Description	Date	Engine: capacity	cylinders*
Kurogane	Type 95	Truck, 200kg, pick-up, 4x4	1936	1,399cc	V2

Soviet Union

Make	Model	Description	Date	Engine: capacity	cylinders*
GAZ	64	Field car, four seater, 4x4	1941	3,280cc	4
	67, 67B	Field car, four seater, 4x4	1942	3,280cc	4

United States of America

Make	Model	Description	Date	Engine: capacity	cylinders*
Bantam	40-BRC	Truck, $\frac{1}{4}$ ton, command reconnaissance, 4x4	1941	1,835cc	4
Crosley	CT-3 Pup	Truck, $\frac{1}{4}$ ton, extra light, 4x4	1943	623cc	H2
Ford	21C	Truck, $\frac{1}{2}$ ton, pick-up, 4x2	1942	3,622cc	V8
	2GC	Truck, $\frac{1}{2}$ ton, carryall, 4x2	1942	3,703cc	6
	2GC	Truck, $\frac{1}{2}$ ton, pick-up, 4x2	1942	3,703cc	6
	GP	Truck, $\frac{1}{4}$ ton, command reconnaissance, 4x4	1941	1,950cc	4
	GPW	Truck, $\frac{1}{4}$ ton, utility, 4x4	1941	2,199cc	4
Willys-Overland	MA	Truck, $\frac{1}{4}$ ton, utility, 4x4	1941	2,199cc	4
	MB	Truck, $\frac{1}{4}$ ton, utility, 4x4	1941	2,199cc	4

* V = cylinders in Vee formation; H = flat or horizontally-opposed configuration.

Light Trucks, up to 2 tons

Make	Model	Description	Date	Engine: capacity	cylinders*
Australia					
Ford	01T	Truck, 30cwt, GS, 4x2	1940	3,917cc	V8
Chevrolet	C15A	Truck, 15cwt, 4x4	1942	3,548cc	6
	1500	Truck, 30cwt, water tank, 4x2	1941	3,548cc	6
Canada					
Chevrolet	C8A	Truck, 8cwt, GS/personnel, 4x2	1940	3,548cc	6
	C8A	Truck, 8cwt, wireless, 4x2	1940	3,548cc	6
	C8AX	Truck, 8cwt, GS, 4x4	1942	3,548cc	6
	C15	Truck, 15cwt, GS/personnel, 4x2	1940	3,548cc	6
	C15A 8444	Truck, 15cwt, battery charging, 4x4	1942	3,548cc	6
	C15A 8444	Truck, 15cwt, GS, 4x4	1942	3,548cc	6
	C15A 8444	Truck, 15cwt, radio location, 4x4	1942	3,548cc	6
	C15A 8444	Truck, 15cwt, water tank, 200 gal, 4x4	1942	3,548cc	6
	C15A 8444	Truck, 15cwt, wireless, 4x4	1942	3,548cc	6
	C30 8441	Truck, 30cwt, GS, 4x4	1940	3,548cc	6
	MCP 1533X2	Truck, 30cwt, GS, 4x2	1941	3,548cc	6
Dodge	T212 D8A	Truck, 8cwt, GS/personnel, 4x4	1941	3,572cc	6
	T222 D15	Truck, 15cwt, GS, 4x2	1944	3,877cc	6
	T222 D15	Truck, 15cwt, water tank, 200 gallon, 4x2	1944	3,877cc	6
	T236 D3/4APT	Truck, 3/4 ton, GS, APT, 4x4; WC52	1944	3,877cc	6
Ford	F8	Truck, 8cwt, GS/personnel, 4x2	1940	3,917cc	V8
	F8A	Truck, 8cwt, GS/personnel, 4x4	1940	3,917cc	V8
	F15A CO11WQF	Truck, 15cwt, battery charging, 4x4	1940	3,917cc	V8
	F15A CO11WQF	Truck, 15cwt, cable layer, 4x4	1940	3,917cc	V8
	F15A CO11WQF	Truck, 15cwt, GS, 4x4	1940	3,917cc	V8
	F15A CO11WQF	Truck, 15cwt, machinery, 4x4	1940	3,917cc	V8
	F15A CO11WQF	Truck, 15cwt, office, 4x4	1940	3,917cc	V8
	F15A CO11WQF	Truck, 15cwt, radio location, 4x4	1940	3,917cc	V8
	F15A CO11WQF	Truck, 15cwt, van, 4x4	1940	3,917cc	V8
	F15A CO11WQF	Truck, 15cwt, wireless, 4x4	1940	3,917cc	V8
	F30 C29QF	Truck, 30cwt, GS, 4x4	1940	3,917cc	V8
Germany					
Adler	W60/61	Truck, light, cargo, 4x2	1937	2,499cc	6
	D7	Truck, light, 1 ton, half-track; SdKfz10	1940	4,198cc	6
Austro-Daimler	ADGR	Truck, light, personnel, 6x4 (Austrian)	1936	2,260cc	6
Auto Union	1500A/02	Truck, light, 4x4	1941	3,517cc	V8
Borgward	B1000	Truck, light, cargo, 4x2	1943	1,384cc	4
	le.gl.E.Lkw	Truck, light, 6x6	1937	6,234cc	6 (D)
Büssing-NAG	D7	Truck, light, 1 ton, half-track; SdKfz10	1939	4,198cc	6
	G31	Truck, light, 6x4	1931	3,920cc	4
	le.gl.E.Lkw	Truck, light, 6x6	1937	6,234cc	6 (D)
Citroen	T23U	Truck, light, cargo, 4x2 (French)	1935	1,911cc	4
	T23RU	Truck, light, cargo, 4x2 (French)	1941	1,911cc	4
Demag	DII 3	Truck, light, 1 ton, half-track	1936	1,971cc	4
	D6	Truck, light, 1 ton, half-track	1937	3,790cc	6
	D7	Truck, light, 1 ton, half-track; SdKfz10	1938	4,198cc	6

* V = cylinders in Vee formation; H = flat or horizontally-opposed configuration.

Make	Model	Description	Date	Engine: capacity	cylinders*
FAUN	le.gl.E.Lkw	Truck, light, 6x6	1937	6,234cc	6 (D)
Hansa-Lloyd	le.gl.E.Lkw	Truck, light, 6x6	1937	6,234cc	6 (D)
Henschel	le.gl.E.Lkw	Truck, light, 6x6	1937	6,234cc	6 (D)
KHD	le.gl.E.Lkw	Truck, light, 6x6	1937	6,234cc	6 (D)
Krupp	L2H43	Truck, light, 6x4	1934	3,308cc	4
	L2H143	Truck, light, 6x4	1937	3,308cc	4
Magirus	le.gl.E.Lkw	Truck, light, 6x6	1937	6,234cc	6 (D)
	M206	Truck, light, engineers, 6x4	1934	4,562cc	6 (D)
MAN	le.gl.E.Lkw	Truck, light, 6x6	1937	6,234cc	6 (D)
Mercedes-Benz	le.gl.E.Lkw	Truck, light, 6x6	1937	6,234cc	6 (D)
	G3A	Truck, light, 6x4, cargo	1929	3,663cc	6
	L1500A	Truck, light, cargo, 4x4	1941	2,594cc	6
	L1500S	Truck, light, cargo, 4x2	1941	2,594cc	6
MWC	D7	Truck, light, 1 ton, half-track; SdKfz10	1943	4,198cc	6
Opel	Blitz 2.5-32	Truck, light, cargo, 4x2	1938	2,473cc	6
	Blitz 3.6-36S	Truck, 2 ton, cargo, half-track; SdKfz3	1937	3,626cc	6
Phänomen	Granit 1500A	Truck, light, 4x4	1940	2,678cc	4
	Granit 1500S	Truck, light, 4x2	1940	2,678cc	4
Praga	RV	Truck, light, cargo, 6x4 (Czech)	1935	3,468cc	6
	RVR	Truck, light, radio, 6x4 (Czech)	1935	3,468cc	6
Renault	AHS	Truck, light, cargo, 4x2 (French)	1941	2,383cc	4
Saurer	D7	Truck, light, 1 ton, half-track; SdKfz10	1938	4,198cc	6
Steyr	640	Truck, light, cargo, 6x4 (Austrian)	1937	2,260cc	6
	1500A/02	Truck, light, 4x4 (Austrian)	1941	3,517cc	V8
Tatra	T92, T93	Truck, 2 ton, cargo, 6x4 (Czech)	1938	3,981cc	V8
Wikov	MNO	Truck, 1½ ton, cargo, 4x2 (Czech)	1937	1,940cc	4
Great Britain					
Albion	AM463	Truck, 2 ton, refueller, 350 gallon, 4x2	1934	4,427cc	4
Austin	BYD	Truck, 15cwt, GS, 4x2	1940	1,861cc	4
	K30/YC	Truck, 30cwt, GS, 4x2	1940	3,462cc	6
	K2A	Truck, 2 ton, GS, 4x2	1944	3,462cc	6
Bedford	JCV	Van, 10-12cwt, 4x2	1939	1,442cc	4
	MWD	Truck, 15cwt, GS, 4x2	1936	3,519cc	6
	MWW	Truck, 15cwt, van, 4x2	1936	3,519cc	6
	MWC	Truck, 15cwt, water tank, 200 gallon, 4x2	1936	3,519cc	6
	MWR	Truck, 15cwt, wireless, 4x2	1936	3,519cc	6
	K	Truck, 30-40cwt	1939	3,519cc	6
	MSC	Truck, 30cwt, GS, 4x2	1939	3,519cc	6
	MSC	Truck, 30cwt, tipper, 4x2	1939	3,519cc	6
	OXD	Truck, 30cwt, GS, 4x2	1939	3,519cc	6
	OXC	Truck, 30 cwt, mobile canteen, 4x2	1939	3,519cc	6
	ML	Truck, 2-3 ton, GS, 4x2	1939	3,519cc	6
	ML	Truck, 2-3 ton, petrol, 800 gallon, 4x2	1939	3,519cc	6
	ML	Truck, 2-3 ton, tipper, 4x2	1939	3,519cc	6
	MS	Truck, 2-3 ton, tipper, 4x2	1939	3,519cc	6
Commer	Beetle	Truck, 15cwt, GS, 4x2	1935	3,040cc	6
	Q2	Truck, 15cwt, aircraft pre-heater, 4x2	1940	3,180cc	6

* V = cylinders in Vee formation; H = flat or horizontally-opposed configuration.

Left: 30cwt Bedford OXC tractor unit. The OXC was equipped with a Scammell trailer coupling and was intended for use with a range of 6-ton semi-trailers. *(TM)*

Make	Model	Description	Date	Engine: capacity	cylinders*
Commer	Q2	Truck, 15cwt, GS, 4x2	1940	3,180cc	6
(cont)	Q2	Truck, 15cwt, van, 4x2	1940	3,180cc	6
	Q15	Truck, 15cwt, GS, 4x2	1940	1,944cc	4
	Q25	Truck, 25cwt, GS, 4x2	1944	1,944cc	4
	Q2	Truck, 30cwt, explosives, 4x2	1940	3,180cc	6(D)
	Q2	Truck, 30cwt, GS, 4x2	1940	3,180cc	6
	Q2	Truck, 2 ton, tractor, 4x2	1939	4,086cc	6
Dennis	AM30/40	Truck, 30-40cwt, GS, 4x2	1940	3,770cc	4
	AM30/40	Truck, 30-40cwt, tractor, 4x2	1940	3,770cc	4
Ford	WOC1	Truck, 8cwt, GS, 4x2	1939	3,621cc	V8
	WOC1	Truck, 8cwt, wireless, 4x2	1939	3,621cc	V8
	WOT2E, 2F	Truck, 15cwt, GS, 4x2	1939	3,621cc	V8
	E01Y	Truck, 15cwt, van, 4x2	1940	3,621cc	V8
	WOT2B	Truck, 15cwt, van, 4x2	1939	3,621cc	V8
	E018T	Truck, 30cwt, GS, 4x2	1940	3,621cc	V8
	WOT3D	Truck, 30cwt, GS, 4x2	1939	3,621cc	V8
	WOT8	Truck, 30cwt, GS, 4x4	1941	3,621cc	V8
	WOT3D	Truck, 30cwt, workshop, 4x2	1939	3,621cc	V8
Guy	Ant	Truck, 15cwt, GS, 4x2	1935	3,686cc	4
	Quad Ant	Truck, 15cwt, GS, 4x4	1938	3,686cc	4
Humber	FWD	Truck, 8cwt, GS, 4x4	1940	4,086cc	6
	FWD	Truck, 8cwt, wireless, 4x4	1940	4,086cc	6
	Snipe	Truck, 8cwt, GS, 4x2	1939	4,086cc	6
Morris-Commercial	PU Mk 2	Truck, 8cwt, GS, 4x2	1936	3,480cc	6
	PU Mk 2	Truck, 8cwt, wireless, 4x2	1936	3,480cc	6
	PU8/4	Truck, 8cwt, GS, 4x4	1942	3,480cc	6
	PU8/4	Truck, 8cwt, wireless, 4x4	1942	3,480cc	6
	C4	Truck, 15cwt, GS, 4x2	1942	3,519cc	4
	C4	Truck, 15cwt, wireless, 4x2	1942	3,519cc	4
	C8	Truck, 15cwt, GS, 4x4	1944	3,494cc	4

* V = cylinders in Vee formation; H = flat or horizontally-opposed configuration.

Make	Model	Description	Date	Engine: capacity	cylinders*
	C8/P	Carrier, 15cwt, SP, predictor, 4x4	1938	3,519cc	4
	CS8	Truck, 15cwt, air compressor, 4x2	1934	3,485cc	6
	CS8	Truck, 15cwt, GS, 4x2	1934	3,485cc	6
	CS8	Truck, 15cwt, office, 4x2	1934	3,485cc	6
	CS8	Truck, 15cwt, wireless, 4x2	1934	3,485cc	6
	CD	Truck, 30cwt, GS, 6x4	1933	3,519cc	4
	CDF, CDFW	Truck, 30cwt, GS, 6x4	1934	3,519cc	4
	CDF, CDFW	Truck, 30cwt, office, 6x4	1934	3,519cc	4
	C11/30	Truck, 30cwt, GS, 4x2	1935	3,519cc	4
	CS11/30	Truck, 30cwt, GS, 4x2	1935	3,485cc	6
Thornycroft	GF/TC4	Truck, 30cwt, GS, 4x2	1939	3,865cc	4
	GF/TC4	Truck, 30cwt, tipper, 4x2	1939	3,865cc	4
	HF/TC4	Truck, 30cwt, GS, 4x2	1939	3,865cc	4

India

Make	Model	Description	Date	Engine: capacity	cylinders*
Chevrolet	1311X3	Truck, 15cwt, GS, 4x4	1939	3,540cc	6
Ford	11C	Truck, 15cwt, GS, 4x4	1941	3,621cc	V8

Italy

Make	Model	Description	Date	Engine: capacity	cylinders*
Fiat	508 Camioncino	Truck, light, 350kg, cargo, 4x2	1934	995cc	4
	508L 'Col/Mil'	Truck, light, 600kg, cargo, 4x2	1939	1,090cc	4
	618M 'Col'	Truck, light, 1300kg, cargo, 4x2	1934	1,944cc	4
OM	Autocarretta 32	Truck, light, cargo, 4x4	1932	1,616cc	4
	Autocarretta 36	Truck, light, cargo, 4x4	1936	1,616cc	4
	Autocarretta 37	Truck, light, cargo, 4x4	1937	1,616cc	4
SPA	AS37, TL37	Truck, light, 1000kg, 4x4	1937	4,053cc	4
	CL39, CL39 'Col'	Truck, light, 1000kg, cargo, 4x2	1939	1,628cc	4
	CLF39	Truck, light, infantry, 4x2	1939	1,628cc	4
	Dovunque 33	Truck, light, cargo, 6x4	1932	2,953cc	4

Japan

Make	Model	Description	Date	Engine: capacity	cylinders*
Isuzu	Type 94A	Truck, 1½ ton, cargo, 4x2	1934	4,390cc	6
	Type 94A	Truck, 1½ ton, airfield tanker, 6x4	1934	4,390cc	6
	Type 94A	Truck, 1½ ton, cargo/personnel, 6x4	1934	4,390cc	6
	Type 94B	Truck, 1½ ton, cargo/personnel, 6x4	1934	4,840cc	4 (D)
	Type 97	Truck, 2 ton, cargo, 4x2	1937	4,390cc	6
	ROK1	Truck, 2 ton, cargo, 6x6	1942	4,390cc	6
	TX40	Truck, 2 ton, cargo, 4x2	1939	4,390cc	6
	YOK1	Truck, 2 ton, cargo, 4x4	1942	4,390cc	6
Nissan	80	Truck, 1½ ton, cargo, 4x2	1938	3,670cc	6
	180	Truck, 1½ ton, cargo, 4x2	1941	3,670cc	6
Toyota	AK10	Truck, 15cwt, cargo, 4x2	1936	3,389cc	6
	G1	Truck, 1½ ton, cargo, 4x2	1935	3,400cc	6
	GA	Truck, 1½ ton, cargo, 4x2	1936	3,400cc	6
	GB	Truck, 1½ ton, cargo, 4x2	1938	3,400cc	6
	KB	Truck, 1½ ton, cargo, 4x2	1938	3,389cc	6
	KC	Truck, 1½ ton, cargo, 4x2	1941	3,389cc	6

* V = cylinders in Vee formation; H = flat or horizontally-opposed configuration.

Make	Model	Description	Date	Engine: capacity	cylinders*
Soviet Union					
GAZ	AA	Truck, $1\frac{1}{2}$ ton, cargo, 4x2	1932	3,285cc	4
	AAA	Truck, $1\frac{1}{2}$ ton, cargo, 6x4	1933	3,285cc	4
	MM-V	Truck, $1\frac{1}{2}$ ton, cargo, 6x4	1941	3,285cc	4
	60	Truck, $1\frac{1}{2}$ ton, cargo, half track	1933	3,285cc	4
GAZ-VM	Pikap	Truck, $\frac{1}{2}$ ton, cargo, half-track	1936	3,285cc	4
ZIS	33	Truck, 2 ton, cargo, half-track	1938	5,522cc	6
United States of America					
Chevrolet	AG	Truck, $\frac{1}{2}$ ton, sedan delivery, 4x2	1941	3,548cc	6
	AK 3104	Truck, $\frac{1}{2}$ ton, canopy express, 4x2	1941	3,548cc	6
	AK 3104	Truck, $\frac{1}{2}$ ton, carryall, 4x2	1941	3,548cc	6
	AK 3104	Truck, $\frac{1}{2}$ ton, panel delivery, 4x2	1941	3,548cc	6
	AK 3104	Truck, $\frac{1}{2}$ ton, pick-up, 4x2	1941	3,548cc	6
	AK 3104	Truck, $\frac{1}{2}$ ton, telephone maintenance, 4x2	1941	3,548cc	6
	AL 3604	Truck, $\frac{1}{2}$ ton, carryall, 4x2	1941	3,548cc	6
	AL 3605	Truck, $\frac{1}{2}$ ton, panel delivery, 4x2	1941	3,548cc	6
	AL 3604	Truck, $\frac{1}{2}$ ton, pick-up, 4x2	1941	3,548cc	6
	AL 3605	Truck, $\frac{1}{2}$ ton, telephone maintenance, 4x2	1941	3,548cc	6
	BK 3104	Truck, $\frac{1}{2}$ ton, canopy express, 4x2	1942	3,548cc	6
	BK 3104	Truck, $\frac{1}{2}$ ton, carryall, 4x2	1942	3,548cc	6
	BK 3104	Truck, $\frac{1}{2}$ ton, panel delivery, 4x2	1942	3,548cc	6
	BK 3104	Truck, $\frac{1}{2}$ ton, pick-up, 4x2	1942	3,548cc	6
	BL 3605	Truck, $\frac{1}{2}$ ton, panel delivery, 4x2	1942	3,548cc	6
	BL 3604	Truck, $\frac{1}{2}$ ton, pick-up, 4x2	1942	3,548cc	6
	KB	Truck, $\frac{1}{2}$ ton, sedan delivery, 4x2	1940	3,548cc	6
	KC	Truck, $\frac{1}{2}$ ton, canopy express, 4x2	1940	3,548cc	6
	KC	Truck, $\frac{1}{2}$ ton, carryall, 4x2	1940	3,548cc	6
	KC	Truck, $\frac{1}{2}$ ton, panel delivery, 4x2	1940	3,548cc	6
	KC, KD, KE	Truck, $\frac{1}{2}$ ton, pick-up, 4x2	1940	3,548cc	6
	MR	Truck, $1\frac{1}{2}$ ton, canopy express, 4x2	1941	3,548cc	6
	MR	Truck, $1\frac{1}{2}$ ton, cargo, 4x2	1941	3,548cc	6
	MR	Truck, $1\frac{1}{2}$ ton, dump, 4x2	1941	3,548cc	6
	MR	Truck, $1\frac{1}{2}$ ton, panel delivery, 4x2	1941	3,548cc	6
	MR	Truck, $1\frac{1}{2}$ ton, pick-up, 4x2	1941	3,548cc	6
	MR	Truck, $1\frac{1}{2}$ ton, stake/platform, 4x2	1941	3,548cc	6
	MR	Truck, $1\frac{1}{2}$ ton, tanker, 500 gallon, 4x2	1941	3,548cc	6
	MR	Truck, $1\frac{1}{2}$ ton, tractor, 4x2	1941	3,548cc	6
	MS	Truck, $1\frac{1}{2}$ ton, dump, 4x2	1942	3,548cc	6
	WA	Truck, $1\frac{1}{2}$ ton, cargo, 4x2	1940	3,548cc	6
	WA	Truck, $1\frac{1}{2}$ ton, canopy express, 4x2	1940	3,548cc	6
	WA	Truck, $1\frac{1}{2}$ ton, dump, 4x2	1940	3,548cc	6
	WA	Truck, $1\frac{1}{2}$ ton, panel delivery, 4x2	1940	3,548cc	6
	WA	Truck, $1\frac{1}{2}$ ton, pick-up, 4x2	1940	3,548cc	6
	WA	Truck, $1\frac{1}{2}$ ton, stake/platform, 4x2	1940	3,548cc	6
	WA	Truck, $1\frac{1}{2}$ ton, tractor, 4x2	1940	3,548cc	6
	WB	Truck, $1\frac{1}{2}$ ton, stake/platform, 4x2	1940	3,548cc	6
	YR	Truck, $1\frac{1}{2}$ ton, cargo, 4x2	1941	3,548cc	6

* V = cylinders in Vee formation; H = flat or horizontally-opposed configuration.

Make	Model	Description	Date	Engine: capacity	cylinders*
Chevrolet (cont)	YR	Truck, 1¹/₂ ton, canopy express, 4x2	1941	3,548cc	6
	YR	Truck, 1¹/₂ ton, dump, 4x2	1941	3,548cc	6
	YR	Truck, 1¹/₂ ton, panel delivery, 4x2	1941	3,548cc	6
	YR	Truck, 1¹/₂ ton, pick-up, 4x2	1940	3,548cc	6
	YR	Truck, 1¹/₂ ton, stake/platform, 4x2	1941	3,548cc	6
	YS	Truck, 1¹/₂ ton, stake/platform, 4x2	1941	3,548cc	6
	G4112 YP	Truck, 1¹/₂ ton, cargo, 4x4	1940	3,859cc	6
	G7107 NJ	Truck, 1¹/₂ ton, cargo, 4x4	1942	3,859cc	6
	G4163 ZP	Truck, 1¹/₂ ton, cargo, 4x4	1940	3,859cc	6
	G7117 NW	Truck, 1¹/₂ ton, cargo, 4x4	1942	3,859cc	6
	G4112 YQ	Truck, 1¹/₂ ton, cargo, LWB, 4x4	1941	3,859cc	6
	G4113 ZP	Truck, 1¹/₂ ton, cargo, LWB, 4x4	1941	3,859cc	6
	G7127 NP	Truck, 1¹/₂ ton, cargo, LWB, 4x4	1942	3,859cc	6
	G7107 YJ	Truck, 1¹/₂ ton, cargo, airborne, 4x4	1941	3,859cc	6
	G4112 YP	Truck, 1¹/₂ ton, dump, 4x4	1940	3,859cc	6
	G7106 NH	Truck, 1¹/₂ ton, dump, 4x4	1940	3,859cc	6
	G7116 NL	Truck, 1¹/₂ ton, dump, 4x4	1942	3,859cc	6
	G7163 NR	Truck, 1¹/₂ ton, earth auger, 4x4; M1	1942	3,859cc	6
	G7163 NR	Truck, 1¹/₂ ton, earth borer and pole setter, 4x4; K-44	1942	3,859cc	6
	G4112 NF	Truck, 1¹/₂ ton, field lighting, 4x4; J3, 4, 5	1940	3,859cc	6
	G4112 ZP	Truck, 1¹/₂ ton, oil servicing, 4x4	1941	3,859cc	6
	G4112 YP	Truck, 1¹/₂ ton, panel delivery, 4x4	1940	3,859cc	6
	G7105 NG	Truck, 1¹/₂ ton, panel delivery, 4x4	1942	3,859cc	6
	G4105 ZP	Truck, 1¹/₂ ton, panel delivery, 4x4	1940	3,859cc	6
	G4100 NG	Truck, 1¹/₂ ton, panel delivery, 4x4; K-51	1940	3,859cc	6
	G4100 ZQ	Truck, 1¹/₂ ton, stake/platform, 15ft, 4x4	1941	3,859cc	6
	G4409 YS	Truck, 1¹/₂ ton, stake/platform, 4x4	1940	3,859cc	6
	G7123 NN	Truck, 1¹/₂ ton, stake/platform, 4x4	1940	3,859cc	6
	G4112 NS	Truck, 1¹/₂ ton, telephone construction, 4x4; K-43	1940	3,859cc	6
	G7173 NN	Truck, 1¹/₂ ton, telephone construction, 4x4; K-43	1942	3,859cc	6
	G4112/G7100 YP	Truck, 1¹/₂ ton, telephone maintenance, 4x4; K-42	1940	3,859cc	6
	G4112 YP	Truck, 1¹/₂ ton, tractor, 4x4	1940	3,859cc	6
	G4103 YR	Truck, 1¹/₂ ton, tractor, 4x4	1941	3,859cc	6
	G4165 ZP	Truck, 1¹/₂ ton, tractor, 4x4	1940	3,859cc	6
	G7113 NK	Truck, 1¹/₂ ton, tractor, 4x4	1942	3,859cc	6
	G7100 YP	Truck, 1¹/₂ ton, turret trainer, 4x4; E-5	1940	3,859cc	6
	G4103 YX	Truck, 1¹/₂ ton, stake/platform, COE; 4x4; K-33, 54	1941	3,859cc	6
	G7123 NN	Truck, 1¹/₂ ton, stake/platform, COE; 4x4; K-33, 54	1942	3,859cc	6
Diamond T	Model 201-S	Truck, ¹/₂ ton, ammunition, 4x2	1941	4,310cc	6
	Model 404-H, S	Truck, 1¹/₂ ton, ammunition, 4x2	1940	4,310cc	6
Dodge	B1B108	Truck, ¹/₂ ton, pick-up, 4x2	1940	3,572cc	6
	T116	Truck, ¹/₂ ton, carryall, 4x2	1942	3,540cc	6

* V = cylinders in Vee formation; H = flat or horizontally-opposed configuration.

Make	Model	Description	Date	Engine: capacity	cylinders*
Dodge (cont)	T116-WD	Truck, ¹/₂ ton, panel delivery, 4x2	1942	3,540cc	6
	T112-WC36, 48	Truck, ¹/₂ ton, panel delivery, 4x2	1941	3,294cc	6
	T202-VC6	Truck, ¹/₂ ton, carryall, 4x4	1939	3,294cc	6
	T202-VC4, 5	Truck, ¹/₂ ton, pick-up, 4x4	1939	3,294cc	6
	T207-VC3	Truck, ¹/₂ ton, pick-up, 4x4	1939	3,294cc	6
	T207-WC10	Truck, ¹/₂ ton, carryall, 4x4	1941	3,567cc	6
	T207-WC11	Truck, ¹/₂ ton, panel delivery, 4x4	1941	3,567cc	6
	T211-WC1	Truck, ¹/₂ ton, pick-up, 4x4	1941	3,567cc	6
	T211-WC3, 4, 5	Truck, ¹/₂ ton, weapons carrier, 4x4	1941	3,567cc	6
	T211-WC17	Truck, ¹/₂ ton, carryall, 4x4	1941	3,769cc	6
	T211-WC12, 13, 14	Truck, ¹/₂ ton, pick-up, 4x4	1941	3,769cc	6
	T211-WC19	Truck, ¹/₂ ton, panel delivery, 4x4	1941	3,769cc	6
	T211-WC20	Truck, ¹/₂ ton, emergency repair, 4x4	1941	3,769cc	6
	T211-WC20	Truck, ¹/₂ ton, oil servicing, 4x4	1941	3,769cc	6
	T215-WC26	Truck, ¹/₂ ton, carryall, 4x4	1941	3,772cc	6
	T215-WC21, 22	Truck, ¹/₂ ton, weapons carrier, 4x4	1941	3,772cc	6
	T215-WC40	Truck, ¹/₂ ton, pick-up, 4x4	1941	3,772cc	6
	T215-WC41	Truck, ¹/₂ ton, emergency repair, 4x4	1941	3,772cc	6
	T215-WC42	Truck, ¹/₂ ton, panel radio, 4x4	1941	3,772cc	6
	T215-WC43	Truck, ¹/₂ ton, telephone maintenance, 4x4	1941	3,772cc	6
	T214-WC51, 52	Truck, ³/₄ ton, weapons carrier, 4x4	1942	3,772cc	6
	T214-WC53	Truck, ³/₄ ton, carryall, 4x4	1942	3,772cc	6
	T214-WC59	Truck, ³/₄ ton, light maintenance, 4x4	1942	3,772cc	6
	T214-WC60	Truck, ³/₄ ton, emergency repair; M2, 4x4	1942	3,772cc	6
	T223-WC62, 63	Truck, 1¹/₂ ton, cargo/personnel, 6x6	1942	3,654cc	6
	T203-VF405	Truck, 1¹/₂ ton, GS, 4x4	1940	3,950cc	6
	T98	Truck, 1¹/₂ ton, cargo, 4x2	1940	3,880cc	6
	T118	Truck, 1¹/₂ ton, tractor, 4x2	1941	3,880cc	6
Ford	21C	Truck, ¹/₂ ton, pick-up, 4x2	1942	3,622cc	V8
	2GC	Truck, ¹/₂ ton, pick-up, 4x2	1941	3,687cc	6
	01W86	Truck, 1¹/₂ ton, stake/platform, 4x2	1940	3,622cc	V8
	018T	Truck, 1¹/₂ ton, stake/platform, 4x2	1940	3,622cc	V8
	01T	Truck, 1¹/₂ ton, cargo, 4x2	1940	3,622cc	V8
	01T	Truck, 1¹/₂ ton, dump, 4x2	1940	3,622cc	V8
	094T	Truck, 1¹/₂ ton, cargo, 4x2	1940	3,622cc	V8
	11T	Truck, 1¹/₂ ton, cargo	1941	3,622cc	V8
	11W	Truck, 1¹/₂ ton, panel delivery, 4x2	1941	3,622cc	V8
	19T	Truck, 1¹/₂ ton, dump, 4x2	1941	3,622cc	V8
	19T	Truck, 1¹/₂ ton, stake/platform, 4x2	1941	3,622cc	V8
	29T80	Truck, 1¹/₂ ton, platform, 4x2	1942	3,622cc	V8
	29W	Truck, 1¹/₂ ton, welding shop, aviation, COE, 4x2	1940	3,622cc	V8
	2G8T	Truck, 1¹/₂ ton, cargo, 4x2	1942	3,622cc	V8
	2G8T	Truck, 1¹/₂ ton, stake/platform, 4x2	1942	3,622cc	V8
	2G8T	Truck, 1¹/₂ ton, stake/platform, LWB, 4x2	1942	3,622cc	V8
	2G8T	Truck, 1¹/₂ ton, tractor, 4x2	1942	3,622cc	V8
	2G8TA	Truck, 1¹/₂ ton, stake/platform, 4x2	1944	3,703cc	6
	2G8TA	Truck, 1¹/₂ ton, tractor, 4x2	1942	3,703cc	6
	2GT	Truck, 1¹/₂ ton, dump, 4x2	1942	3,703cc	6

* V = cylinders in Vee formation; H = flat or horizontally-opposed configuration.

Make	Model	Description	Date	Engine: capacity	cylinders*
Ford	2GT	Truck, $1\frac{1}{2}$ ton, stake/platform, 4x2	1942	3,703cc	6
(cont)	2GT	Truck, $1\frac{1}{2}$ ton, tractor, 4x2	1942	3,703cc	6
	E018T	Truck, $1\frac{1}{2}$ ton, cargo, 4x2	1940	3,622cc	V8
	GTB	Truck, $1\frac{1}{2}$ ton, cargo, 4x4	1942	3,703cc	6
Ford/Marmon	09T	Truck, $1\frac{1}{2}$ ton, cargo, 4x4	1940	3,622cc	V8
	09W	Truck, $1\frac{1}{2}$-3 ton, air compressor, 4x4	1940	3,622cc	V8
	81Y/MH OT2-4	Truck, 1 ton, cargo, 4x4	1938	3,622cc	V8
	51/MH B5-4	Truck, $1\frac{1}{2}$ ton, cargo, 4x4	1935	3,622cc	V8
	HH5-4	Truck, $1\frac{1}{2}$ ton, cargo, 4x4	1942	3,917cc	V8
	MM5-4	Truck, $1\frac{1}{2}$ ton, cargo, 4x4	1941	3,917cc	V8
GMC	AC-101	Truck, $\frac{1}{2}$ ton, carryall, 4x2	1940	3,548cc	6
	4272	Truck, $1\frac{1}{2}$ ton, cargo, 4x4	1936	3,377cc	6
	AC-305	Truck, $1\frac{1}{2}$ ton, cargo, 4x2	1940	3,736cc	6
	ACK-353	Truck, $1\frac{1}{2}$ ton, cargo, 4x4	1940	3,736cc	6
	ACX-353	Truck, $1\frac{1}{2}$ ton, cargo, 4x2	1940	3,736cc	6
	ACX-353	Truck, $1\frac{1}{2}$ ton, dump, 4x2	1940	3,736cc	6
	ACX-353	Truck, $1\frac{1}{2}$ ton, tractor, 4x2	1940	3,736cc	6
	AF-361	Truck, $1\frac{1}{2}$ ton, signals van, 4x2	1940	3,736cc	6
	AFX-312	Truck, $1\frac{1}{2}$ ton, panel delivery, COE, 4x2	1940	3,736cc	6
	CC-252	Truck, $1\frac{1}{2}$ ton, pneumatic elevator platform, 4x2	1942	4,064cc	6
	CC-302	Truck, $1\frac{1}{2}$ ton, cargo, 4x2	1942	4,064cc	6
	CC-302	Truck, $1\frac{1}{2}$ ton, dump, 4x2	1942	4,064cc	6
	CCK-353	Truck, $1\frac{1}{2}$ ton, earth auger, 4x4	1941	4,064cc	6
	CF-351	Truck, $1\frac{1}{2}$ ton, signals, COE, 4x2	1940	3,736cc	6
	CF-361	Truck, $1\frac{1}{2}$ ton, signals, COE, 4x2	1940	3,736cc	6
	AFKX-352	Truck, $1\frac{1}{2}$-3 ton, air compressor, 4x4	1940	3,736cc	6
	AFKX-352	Truck, $1\frac{1}{2}$-3 ton, cargo, 4x4	1940	3,736cc	6
	AFKX-352	Truck, $1\frac{1}{2}$-3 ton, ordnance maintenance, 4x4	1940	3,736cc	6
	AC-453	Truck, 2 ton, stake/platform, 4x2	1940	3,736cc	6
International	M-1-4	Truck, $\frac{1}{2}$ ton, pick-up, 4x4	1941	3,818cc	6
	M-1-4	Truck, $\frac{1}{2}$ ton, radio, 4x4	1941	3,818cc	6
	M-2-4	Truck, 1 ton, cargo, 4x4	1942	3,818cc	6
	D30	Truck, $1\frac{1}{2}$ ton, cargo, 4x2	1939	3,818cc	6
	M-3L-4, M3-H-4	Truck, $1\frac{1}{2}$ ton, cargo, 4x4	1941	4,410cc	6
Studebaker	Weasel	Carrier, light cargo, full-track; M28	1943	2,786cc	6
	Weasel	Carrier, light cargo, full-track; M29	1943	2,786cc	6
White-Indiana	86	Truck, $1\frac{1}{2}$ ton, dump, 4x2	1936	4,392cc	6
Willys	MT-Tug	Truck, $\frac{3}{4}$ ton, tractor, 6x6	1943	2,199cc	4

* V = cylinders in Vee formation; H = flat or horizontally-opposed configuration.

Medium Trucks, up to 3 tons

Make	Model	Description	Date	Engine: capacity	
Australia					
Dodge	T110L D60L	Truck, 3 ton, GS, 4x2	1940	3,877cc	6
Ford	118T	Truck, 3 ton, tractor, 4x2	1940	3,622cc	V8
	118T	Tractor, 3 ton, GS, 4x2, with 7 ton semi-trailer	1942	3,622cc	V8
	F60L	Truck, 3 ton, machinery, 4x4	1940	3,917cc	V8
	296T/MH	Truck, 3 ton, tanker, 6x6	1942	3,917cc	V8
	F60S	Truck, 3 ton, tipper, 4x4	1942	3,917cc	V8
GMC	9600 Series	Truck, 3 ton, aircraft refueller, 4x2	1942	4,416cc	6
International	K7	Tractor, 4x2, 3 ton, with 7 ton semi-trailer, GS	1942	7,391cc	6
Canada					
Chevrolet	CC60L 1543X2	Truck, 3 ton, GS, 4x2	1940	3,548cc	6
	CC60L 1543X2	Truck, 3 ton, stores, 4x2	1940	3,548cc	6
	CC60L 1543X2	Truck, 3 ton, workshop, 4x2	1940	3,548cc	6
	C60S	Truck, 3 ton, power auger, 4x4	1940	3,548cc	6
	C60S	Truck, 3 ton, signal construction, 4x4	1940	3,548cc	6
	C60S	Truck, 3 ton, signals, 4x4	1940	3,548cc	6
	C60S	Truck, 3 ton, stores, 4x4	1940	3,548cc	6
	C60S	Truck, 3 ton, tipper, 4x4	1940	3,548cc	6
	C60S	Truck, 3 ton, wireless, 4x4	1940	3,548cc	6
	C60L 8443	Truck, 3 ton, battery storage, 4x4	1940	3,548cc	6
	C60L 8443	Truck, 3 ton, caravan, 4x4	1940	3,548cc	6
	C60L 8443	Truck, 3 ton, cipher office, 4x4	1940	3,548cc	6
	C60L 8443	Truck, 3 ton, command, high power, 4x4	1940	3,548cc	6
	C60L 8443	Truck, 3 ton, command, low power, 4x4	1940	3,548cc	6
	C60L 8443	Truck, 3 ton, disinfector, 4x4	1940	3,548cc	6
	C60L 8443	Truck, 3 ton, GS, 4x4	1940	3,548cc	6
	C60L 8443	Truck, 3 ton, instrument repair, 4x4	1940	3,548cc	6
	C60L 8443	Truck, 3 ton, machinery, 4x4 (various)	1940	3,548cc	6
	C60L 8443	Truck, 3 ton, mobile kitchen, 4x4	1940	3,548cc	6
	C60L 8443	Truck, 3 ton, office, 4x4	1940	3,548cc	6
	C60L 8443	Truck, 3 ton, petrol, 4x4	1940	3,548cc	6
	C60L 8443	Truck, 3 ton, stores, 4x4	1940	3,548cc	6
	C60L 8443	Truck, 3 ton, teleprinter, 4x4	1940	3,548cc	6
	C60L 8443	Truck, 3 ton, telephone exchange, 4x4	1940	3,548cc	6
	C60L 8443	Truck, 3 ton, workshop, 4x4	1940	3,548cc	6
	C60X	Truck, 3 ton, chemical warfare laboratory, 6x6	1944	3,548cc	6
	C60X	Truck, 3 ton, machinery, 6x6 (various)	1944	3,548cc	6
	C60X	Truck, 3 ton, petroleum laboratory, 6x6	1944	3,548cc	6
	C60X	Truck, 3 ton, stores, 6x6	1944	3,548cc	6
	C60X	Truck, 3 ton, switchboard, 6x6	1944	3,548cc	6
Dodge	T110L-6 D60S	Truck, 3 ton, tipper, 4x2	1940	3,877cc	6
	T110L-9 D60L/D	Truck, 3 ton, GS, 4x2	1942	3,877cc	6
	T130	Truck, 3 ton, GS, COE, 4x2	1942	3,877cc	6
	T130	Truck, 3 ton, tractor, COE, 4x2	1942	3,877cc	6
Ford	F602L	Truck, 3 ton, GS, 4x2	1940	3,917cc	V8
	F602S C29WFS	Truck, 3 ton, GS, 4x2	1940	3,917cc	V8

* V = cylinders in Vee formation; H = flat or horizontally-opposed configuration; (D) = diesel engine; (PG) = producer gas engine. * LWB = Long wheelbase.

Make	Model	Description	Date	Engine: capacity	cylinders*
Ford	F60H C010QF	Truck, 3 ton, workshop, 6x4	1942	3,917cc	V8
(cont)	F60L C298QF	Truck, 3 ton, caravan, 4x4	1940	3,917cc	V8
	F60L C298QF	Truck, 3 ton, GS, 4x4	1940	3,917cc	V8
	F60L C298QF	Truck, 3 ton, machinery, 4x4	1940	3,917cc	V8
	F60L C298QF	Truck, 3 ton, mobile kitchen, 4x4	1940	3,917cc	V8
	F60L C298QF	Truck, 3 ton, stores, 4x4	1940	3,917cc	V8
	F60L C298QF	Truck, 3 ton, workshop, 4x4	1940	3,917cc	V8
	F60S C01QF	Truck, 3 ton, GS, 4x4	1940	3,917cc	V8
	F60S C01QF	Truck, 3 ton, power auger, 4x4	1940	3,917cc	V8
	F60S C01QF	Truck, 3 ton, signals, 4x4	1940	3,917cc	V8
	F60S C01QF	Truck, 3 ton, stores, 4x4	1940	3,917cc	V8
	F60T C395Q	Tractor, 4x4, with 6 ton semi-trailer, GS	1943	3,917cc	V8
	FC60L C298QF	Truck, 3 ton, GS, 4x2	1942	3,917cc	V8
	FS60S	Truck, 3 ton, dump, 4x2	1940	3,917cc	V8
	FS60ST	Truck, 3 ton, tractor, 4x2	1940	3,917cc	V8
	EC098T	Truck, 3 ton, aircraft refueller, 4x2	1942	3,917cc	V8
	EC098T	Truck, 3 ton, GS, 4x2	1942	3,917cc	V8
	EC098T	Truck, 3 ton, stores, 4x2	1942	3,917cc	V8
	EC098T	Truck, 3 ton, tipper, 4x2	1942	3,917cc	V8
GMC	C60X 8660	Truck, 3 ton, stores, 6x6	1942	4,416cc	6
	C60X 8660	Truck, 3 ton, van, 6x6	1942	4,416cc	6
Germany					
Austro-Daimler	ADGR	Truck, medium, cargo/personnel, 6x4 (Austrian)	1936	3,915cc	6
Borgward	B3000A/D	Truck, medium, cargo, 4x4	1942	4,962cc	6 (D)
	B3000A/O	Truck, medium, cargo, 4x4	1942	3,745cc	6
	B3000S/O	Truck, medium, cargo, 4x2	1938	3,745cc	6
Büssing-NAG	Burglowe 25	Truck, medium, signals, 4x2	1938	3,920cc	4
	3GL6	Truck, medium, cargo, 6x4	1935	9,348cc	6
Ford	G917T	Truck, medium, cargo, 4x2	1939	3,613cc	V8
	V3000S/G197TS	Truck, medium, cargo, 4x2	1939	3,613cc	V8
	V3000S/G198TS	Truck, medium, cargo, 4x2	1941	3,924cc	V8
Hansa Lloyd	Merker IIID	Truck, medium, cargo, 4x2	1936	6,126cc	6 (D)
Henschel	33D1	Truck, medium, cargo, 6x4	1933	10,587cc	6 (D)
	33G1	Truck, medium, cargo, 6x4	1934	10,860cc	6 (D)
KHD	A330	Truck, medium, cargo, 4x4	1941	4,942cc	4 (D)
	A3000	Truck, medium, cargo, 4x4	1941	4,942cc	4 (D)
	S3000/SSM	Truck, medium, cargo, half-track	1942	4,942cc	4 (D)
Krupp	L3H63	Truck, medium, cargo, 6x4	1931	7,542cc	6
	L3H163	Truck, medium, cargo, 6x4	1936	7,542cc	6
MAN	E3000	Truck, medium, cargo, 4x2	1940	4,503cc	4 (D)
Mercedes-Benz	L3000A	Truck, medium, cargo, 4x4	1939	4,849cc	4 (D)
	L3000S/O66	Truck, medium, cargo, 4x2	1940	4,849cc	4 (D)
	LG63/LG3000	Truck, medium, cargo, 6x4	1935	7,413cc	6 (D)
	LG65/LG3000	Truck, medium, cargo, 6x6	1935	7,413cc	6 (D)
Opel	Blitz 3.6-36S	Truck, medium, cargo, 4x2	1937	3,626cc	6
	Blitz 3.6-6700A	Truck, medium, cargo, 4x4	1940	3,626cc	6
	Blitz 3.6-36/SSM	Truck, medium, cargo, half-track	1942	3,626cc	6

* V = cylinders in Vee formation; H = flat or horizontally-opposed configuration; (D) = diesel engine; (PG) = producer gas engine. * LWB = Long wheelbase.

Make	Model	Description	Date	Engine: capacity	cylinders*
Praga	RV	Truck, 2 ton, cargo, 6x4 (Czech)	1936	3,468cc	6
Renault	AHN	Truck, medium, cargo, 4x2 (French)	1941	4,086cc	6
Skoda	6L	Truck, 2 ton, cargo, 6x6 (Czech)	1936	3,140cc	6
Tatra	27	Truck, 3 ton, cargo, 4x2 (Czech)	1930	4,612cc	4
Great Britain					
AEC	Marshal 644	Truck, 3 ton, GS, 6x4	1939	5,123cc	6
	Marshal 644	Truck, 3 ton, bridging equipment, small box girder, 6x4	1939	5,123cc	6
Albion	BY1	Truck, 3 ton, bridging equipment, folding boat, 6x4	1937	3,890cc	4
	BY1	Truck, 3 ton, bridging equipment, raft unit, 6x4	1937	3,890cc	4
	BY1	Truck, 3 ton, bridging equipment, small box girder, 6x4	1937	3,890cc	4
	BY1	Truck, 3 ton, bridging equipment, trestle/bay unit, 6x4	1937	3,890cc	4
	BY1	Truck, 3 ton, GS, 6x4	1937	3,890cc	4
	BY1	Truck, 3 ton, machinery, 6x4	1937	3,890cc	4
	BY1	Truck, 3 ton, workshop, 6x4	1937	3,890cc	4
	BY3	Truck, 3 ton, bridging equipment, folding boat, 6x4	1940	4,250cc	6
	BY3	Truck, 3 ton, bridging equipment, raft unit, 6x4	1940	4,250cc	6
	BY3	Truck, 3 ton, bridging equipment, small box girder, 6x4	1940	4,250cc	6
	BY3	Truck, 3 ton, bridging equipment, trestle/bay unit, 6x4	1940	4,250cc	6
	BY3	Truck, 3 ton, GS, 6x4	1940	4,250cc	6
	BY5	Truck, 3 ton, bridging equipment, folding boat, 6x4	1941	4,566cc	6
	BY5	Truck, 3 ton, bridging equipment, raft unit, 6x4	1941	4,566cc	6
	BY5	Truck, 3 ton, bridging equipment, small box girder, 6x4	1941	4,566cc	6
	BY5	Truck, 3 ton, bridging equipment, trestle/bay unit, 6x4	1941	4,566cc	6
	BY5	Truck, 3 ton, GS, 6x4	1941	4,566cc	6
	FT11N	Truck, 3 ton, GS, 4x4	1941	4,560cc	6
	FT11N	Truck, 3 ton, machinery, 4x4	1941	4,560cc	6
	KL127	Truck, 3 ton, X ray, 4x2	1935	3,890cc	4
Austin	K3/YB, ZC, ZR	Truck, 3 ton, GS, 4x2	1939	3,462cc	6
	K3/YF	Truck, 3 ton, GS, 6x4	1940	3,995cc	6
	K3/YJ	Truck, 3 ton, wireless, 4x2	1942	3,462cc	6
	K5/ZD, ZK, ZT	Truck, 3 ton, GS, 4x4	1941	3,995cc	6
	K6/A	Truck, 3 ton, balloon winch, 6x4	1944	3,995cc	6
	K6/ZB	Truck, 3 ton, signals, 6x4	1944	3,995cc	6
Bedford	OL	Truck, 3-4 ton, GS, 4x2	1939	3,519cc	6
	OS	Truck, 3-4 ton, tipper, 4x2	1939	3,519cc	6
	OYC	Truck, 3 ton, petrol, 800 gallon, 4x2	1939	3,519cc	6
	OYC	Truck, 3 ton, water, 350 gallon, 4x2	1939	3,519cc	6
	OYD	Truck, 3 ton, GS, 4x2	1939	3,519cc	6
	OYD	Truck, 3 ton, stores, 4x2	1939	3,519cc	6

* V = cylinders in Vee formation; H = flat or horizontally-opposed configuration; (D) = diesel engine; (PG) = producer gas engine. * LWB = Long wheelbase.

Make	Model	Description	Date	Engine: capacity	cylinders*
Bedford	OYD	Truck, 3 ton, workshop, 350gal, 4x2	1939	3,519cc	6
(cont)	QLC	Truck, 3 ton, petrol, 850/950/1,000 gallon, 4x4	1941	3,519cc	6
	QLC	Truck, 3 ton, studio, 4x4	1941	3,519cc	6
	QLC	Truck, 3 ton, switchboard, 4x4	1941	3,519cc	6
	QLD	Truck, 3 ton, GS, 4x4	1941	3,519cc	6
	QLD	Truck, 3 ton, mobile canteen, 4x4	1941	3,519cc	6
	QLD	Truck, 3 ton, mobile kitchen, 4x4	1941	3,519cc	6
	QLD	Truck, 3 ton, observation tower, 4x4	1941	3,519cc	6
	QLD	Truck, 3 ton, tipper, 4x4	1941	3,519cc	6
	QLR	Truck, 3 ton, wireless, 4x4	1941	3,519cc	6
	QLT	Truck, 3 ton, troop carrier, 4x4	1941	3,519cc	6
	QLW	Truck, 3 ton, winch tipper, 4x4	1941	3,519cc	6
	WTH	Truck, 3 ton, tractor, 4x2	1938	3,519cc	6
Commer	Q4	Truck, 3 ton, GS, 4x2	1939	4,086cc	6
	Q4	Truck, 3 ton, workshop, 4x2	1939	4,086cc	6
	Q3	Truck, 4 ton, tractor, 4x2	1939	4,086cc	6
Crossley	FWD Type 1	Truck, 3 ton, tractor, 4x4	1940	5,266cc	4
	IGL8	Truck, 3 ton, GS, 6x4	1938	5,266cc	4
	IGL8	Truck, 3 ton, workshop, 6x4	1938	5,266cc	4
	Q Type	Truck, 3 ton, GS, 4x4	1936	5,266cc	4
	Q Type	Truck, 3 ton, workshop, 4x4	1936	5,266cc	4
Dennis	'Pig'	Truck, 3 ton, tipper, 4x2	1939	3,770cc	6
Dodge ('Kew')	82, 82A	Truck, 3 ton, tipper, 4x2	1940	5,420cc	6
	80B	Truck, 3 ton, workshop, 4x2	1940	5,420cc	6
	-	Truck, 3 ton, balloon winch, 6x4	1940	5,420cc	6
Ford	E917T	Truck, 3 ton, searchlight, 6x4	1940	3,621cc	V8
	WOT1, WOT1A	Truck, 3 ton, balloon winch, 6x4	1940	3,621cc	V8
	WOT1, WOT1A	Truck, 3 ton, floodlight, 6x4	1940	3,621cc	V8
	WOT1, WOT1A	Truck, 3 ton, GS, 6x4	1940	3,621cc	V8
	WOT1, WOT1A	Truck, 3 ton, office, 6x4	1940	3,621cc	V8
	WOT1, WOT1A	Truck, 3 ton, parachute drying, 6x4	1940	3,621cc	V8
	WOT1, WOT1A	Truck, 3 ton, power charging, 6x4	1940	3,621cc	V8
	WOT6	Truck, 3 ton, GS, 4x4	1942	3,621cc	V8
	WOT6	Truck, 3 ton, machinery, 4x4 (various)	1942	3,621cc	V8
Guy	FBAX	Truck, 3 ton, GS, 6x4	1938	5,112cc	6
	FBAX	Truck, 3 ton, searchlight, 6x4	1938	5,112cc	6
	FBAX	Truck, 3 ton, wireless, 6x4	1938	5,112cc	6
	FBAX	Truck, 3 ton, workshop, 6x4	1938	5,112cc	6
	PE	Truck, 3 ton, searchlight, 4x2	1937	3,686cc	6
Karrier	CK6	Truck, 3 ton, bridging equipment, folding boat, 6x4	1935	4,086cc	6
	CK6	Truck, 3 ton, bridging equipment, raft unit, 6x4	1935	4,086cc	6
	CK6	Truck, 3 ton, bridging equipment, small box girder, 6x4	1935	4,086cc	6
	CK6	Truck, 3 ton, GS, 6x4	1935	4,086cc	6
	CK6	Truck, 3 ton, workshop, 6x4	1935	4,086cc	6
	K6	Truck, 3 ton, GS, 4x4	1940	4,086cc	6
Leyland	Lynx WDZ	Truck, 3 ton, GS, 4x2	1939	4,730cc	6
	Retriever WLW3	Truck, 3 ton, bridging equipment, raft unit, 6x4	1939	5,895cc	6

* V = cylinders in Vee formation; H = flat or horizontally-opposed configuration; (D) = diesel engine; (PG) = producer gas engine. * LWB = Long wheelbase.

Left: A Bedford QLR radio truck, in post-war Deep Bronze Green finish. *(ST)*

Make	Model	Description	Date	Engine: capacity	cylinders*
Leyland	Retriever WLW3	Truck, 3 ton, GS, 6x4	1939	5,895cc	6
(cont)	Retriever WLW3	Truck, 3 ton, machinery, 6x4	1939	5,895cc	6
	Retriever WLW3	Truck, 3 ton, searchlight, 6x4	1939	5,895cc	6
	Retriever WLW3	Truck, 3 ton, wireless, 6x4	1939	5,895cc	6
	Retriever WLW3	Truck, 3 ton, workshop, 6x4	1939	5,895cc	6
Thornycroft	Nubian TF/AC4	Truck, 3 ton, GS, 4x4	1940	3,865cc	6
	Sturdy WZ/TC4	Truck, 3 ton, GS, 4x2	1941	3,865cc	6
	Sturdy WZ/TC4	Truck, 3 ton, tipper, 4x2	1941	3,865cc	6
	Tartar WO/AC4	Truck, 3 ton, GS, 6x4	1938	5,173cc	6
	Tartar WO/AC4	Truck, 3 ton, machinery, 6x4	1938	5,173cc	6
	Tartar WO/AC4	Truck, 3 ton, workshop, 6x4	1938	5,173cc	6
	Tartar WOF/AC4	Truck, 3 ton, GS, 6x4	1941	5,173cc	6
	Tartar WOF/DC4	Truck, 3 ton, GS, 6x4	1941	7,436cc	6 (D)
	Tartar WOF/AC4	Truck, 3 ton, machinery, 6x4	1941	5,173cc	6
	Tartar WOF/AC4	Truck, 3 ton, workshop, 6x4	1941	5,173cc	6
	Tartar WOF/DC4	Truck, 3 ton, workshop, 6x4	1941	7,436cc	6 (D)
	ZS/TC4	Truck, 3 ton, generator, water tank, 4x2	1937	3,865cc	6
	ZS/TC4	Truck, 3 ton, parachute servicing, 4x2	1937	3,865cc	6
	ZS/TC4	Truck, 3 ton, searchlight, 4x2	1937	3,865cc	6
Tilling-Stevens	TS19	Truck, 3 ton, searchlight, 4x2	1935	5,115cc	6
	TS20	Truck, 3 ton, searchlight, 4x2	1939	4,576cc	6
	TS20	Truck, 3 ton, workshop, ambulance repair, 4x2	1939	4,576cc	6
Italy					
Alfa Romeo	430RE	Truck, medium, cargo, 4x2	1940	5,816cc	4 (D)
	500RE	Truck, medium, cargo, 4x2	1942	6,125cc	6 (D)
Bianchi	36 Mediolanum	Truck, medium, cargo, 4x2	1935	4,942cc	4 (D)

* V = cylinders in Vee formation; H = flat or horizontally-opposed configuration; (D) = diesel engine; (PG) = producer gas engine. * LWB = Long wheelbase.

Make	Model	Description	Date	Engine: capacity	cylinders*
Bianchi (cont)	68	Truck, medium, cargo, 4x2	1936	4,942cc	4 (D)
	Miles	Truck, medium, cargo, 4x2	1939	4,849cc	4 (D)
Ceirano	47CM	Truck, medium, cargo, 4x2	1931	4,712cc	4
Fiat	621PN	Truck, medium, cargo, 6x4	1934	4,580cc	4 (D)
	626NL	Truck, medium, cargo, 4x2	1941	5,750cc	6 (D)
	626BL	Truck, medium, cargo, 4x2	1941	5,750cc	6
Isotta Fraschini	D70M	Truck, medium, cargo, 4x2	1936	6,754cc	6 (D)
	D65UMB	Truck, medium, cargo, 4x2	1943	5,817cc	4
Lancia	Esaro 267 'Mil'	Truck, medium, cargo, 4x2	1942	6,875cc	5 (D)
OM	1CRD 'Mil'	Truck, medium, cargo, 4x2	1936	4,500cc	4
	Taurus B	Truck, medium, cargo, 4x2	1939	5,320cc	4
	Taurus N	Truck, medium, cargo, 4x2	1939	5,320cc	4 (D)
SPA	38R	Truck, medium, cargo, 4x2	1936	4,053cc	4
	38R	Truck, medium, refrigerated, 4x2	1936	4,053cc	4
	Dovunque 33	Truck, medium, cargo, 6x4	1933	4,053cc	4
	Dovunque 35	Truck, medium, cargo, 6x4	1935	4,053cc	4
	Dovunque 41	Truck, medium, cargo, 6x6	1943	9,365cc	6 (D)
	T40	Truck, medium, cargo, 4x4	1941	9,365cc	6 (D)

Japan

Make	Model	Description	Date	Engine: capacity	cylinders*
Isuzu	TU10	Truck, 3 ton, cargo, 6x4; Type 94A	1934	4,390cc	6
	TU23	Truck, 3 ton, cargo, 6x4; Type 94B	1941	5,100cc	6 (D)

Soviet Union

Make	Model	Description	Date	Engine: capacity	cylinders*
ZIS	22	Truck, 2½ ton, cargo, half-track	1938	5,522cc	6
	22M	Truck, 2½ ton, cargo, half-track	1939	5,522cc	6
	42	Truck, 2½ ton, cargo, half-track	1942	5,522cc	6
	42M	Truck, 2½ ton, cargo, half-track	1942	5,522cc	6
	32	Truck, 2½ ton, cargo, 4x4	1940	5,522cc	6
	6	Truck, 2½ ton, cargo, 6x4	1933	5,522cc	6
	5V	Truck, 3 ton, cargo, 4x2	1933	5,522cc	6
	30	Truck, 3 ton, cargo, 4x2	1940	5,522cc	6

United States of America

Make	Model	Description	Date	Engine: capacity	cylinders*
Autocar	U-2044	Truck, 2½ ton, oil servicing, 660 gallon, COE, 4x4; L-1	1940	5,244cc	6
	U-4044	Truck, 2½ ton, tractor, COE, 4x4	1940	5,244cc	6
	U-4144	Truck, 2½ ton, oil servicing, 660 gallon, COE, 4x4	1941	5,866cc	6
	U-4144T	Truck, 2½ ton, tractor, COE, 4x4	1941	5,866cc	6
Chevrolet-Thornton	YS4103	Truck, 3 ton, GS, 6x4	1941	3,540cc	6
Diamond T	Model 406-H	Truck, 2½ ton, stake/platform, 4x2	1940	5,244cc	6
	Model 509-H, HS	Truck, 2½ ton, ammunition, 4x2	1940	5,244cc	6
	Model 509-H	Truck, 2½ ton, cargo, 4x2	1940	5,244cc	6
	Model 509-H	Truck, 2½ ton, dump, 4x2	1940	5,244cc	6
	Model 509-H, HS	Truck, 2½ ton, stake/platform, 4x2	1940	5,244cc	6
	Model 614	Truck, 2½ ton, cargo, 4x2	1940	5,244cc	6
	Model 614	Truck, 2½ ton, dump, 4x2	1940	5,244cc	6

* V = cylinders in Vee formation; H = flat or horizontally-opposed configuration; (D) = diesel engine; (PG) = producer gas engine. * LWB = Long wheelbase.

Make	Model	Description	Date	Engine: capacity	cylinders*
Diamond T	Model 614	Truck, 2^1/$_2$ ton, line construction, 4x2	1940	5,244cc	6
(cont)	Model 614	Truck, 2^1/$_2$ ton, telephone maintenance, 4x2	1940	5,244cc	6
Dodge	VH48	Truck, 3 ton, cargo, 4x2	1939	3,949cc	6
	T234	Truck, 3 ton, cargo, 4x2	1939	3,949cc	6
	VK62, 62B	Truck, 3 ton, GS, 4x2	1939	5,424cc	6
	T110L-3	Truck, 3 ton, stake body, 4x2	1939	3,870cc	6
Federal	2G	Truck, 2^1/$_2$ ton, dump, 4x2	1943	5,244cc	6
	2G, 3G	Truck, 2^1/$_2$ ton, telephone maintenance, 4x2	1943	5,244cc	6
Ford-Marmon	198T	Truck, 2^1/$_2$ ton, searchlight, 6x6	1941	3,622cc	V8
	198T	Truck, 2^1/$_2$ ton, sound ranging, 6x6	1941	3,622cc	V8
GMC	AC-355	Truck, 2^1/$_2$ ton, stake/platform	1940	4,195cc	6
	ACK-353	Truck, 2^1/$_2$ ton, stake, tire servicing, 4x2	1943	4,195cc	6
	ACKW-353	Truck, 2^1/$_2$ ton, cargo, 6x6	1940	4,195cc	6
	ACKW-353	Truck, 2^1/$_2$ ton, platform, battery service, 6x6	1943	4,195cc	6
	ACKWX-353	Truck, 2^1/$_2$ ton, cargo, 6x6	1940	4,556cc	6
	ACKWX-353	Truck, 2^1/$_2$ ton, platform, battery service, 6x6	1943	4,556cc	6
	ACKWX-353	Truck, 2^1/$_2$ ton, stock rack, 6x6	1940	4,556cc	6
	ACKWX-353	Truck, 2^1/$_2$ ton, tank, 750 gallon, 6x6	1943	4,556cc	6
	ACX-453	Truck, 2^1/$_2$ ton, dump, 4x2	1940	4,416cc	6
	AF502	Truck, 2^1/$_2$ ton, cargo, 4x2	1940	4,416cc	6
	AF503	Truck, 2^1/$_2$ ton, cargo, COE, 4x2	1940	4,416cc	6
	AFKWX-352	Truck, 2^1/$_2$ ton, dump, COE, 6x6	1940	4,416cc	6
	AFKWX-353	Truck, 2^1/$_2$ ton, cargo, COE, 6x6	1940	4,416cc	6
	AFKX-352	Truck, 2^1/$_2$ ton, cargo, COE, 4x4	1940	4,416cc	6
	AFKX-502	Truck, 2^1/$_2$ ton, tractor, 4x4	1940	5,047cc	6
	AFWX-354	Truck, 2^1/$_2$ ton, cargo, COE, 6x4	1940	4,064cc	6
	AFWX-354	Truck, 2^1/$_2$ ton, searchlight, COE, 6x4	1940	4,064cc	6
	AFX-622	Truck, 2^1/$_2$ ton, tractor, COE, 4x2	1940	4,416cc	6
	ACX-503	Truck, 2^1/$_2$ ton, tractor, 4x2	1942	4,416cc	6
	CC-453	Truck, 2^1/$_2$ ton, canopy express, 4x2	1941	4,416cc	6
	CC-453	Truck, 2^1/$_2$ ton, cargo, 4x2	1941	4,416cc	6
	CC-453	Truck, 2^1/$_2$ ton, stake/platform, 4x2	1942	4,416cc	6
	CCKW-352	Truck, 2^1/$_2$ ton, cargo, 6x6	1941	4,416cc	6
	CCKW-352	Truck, 2^1/$_2$ ton, oil servicing, 660 gallon, 6x6; L-2	1941	4,416cc	6
	CCKW-352	Truck, 2^1/$_2$ ton, ordnance maintenance, 6x6	1941	4,416cc	6
	CCKW-353	Truck, 2^1/$_2$ ton, air compressor, 6x6	1941	4,416cc	6
	CCKW-353	Truck, 2^1/$_2$ ton, cargo, 6x6	1941	4,416cc	6
	CCKW-353	Truck, 2^1/$_2$ ton, chemical service, 6x6	1941	4,416cc	6
	CCKW-353	Truck, 2^1/$_2$ ton, decontaminating equipment, 6x6	1941	4,416cc	6
	CCKW-353	Truck, 2^1/$_2$ ton, dump, 6x6	1941	4,416cc	6
	CCKW-353	Truck, 2^1/$_2$ ton, fuel or oil servicing, 6x6; F-3	1941	4,416cc	6
	CCKW-353	Truck, 2^1/$_2$ ton, gasoline, 750 gallon, 6x6	1941	4,416cc	6
	CCKW-353	Truck, 2^1/$_2$ ton, map reproduction, 6x6	1941	4,416cc	6
	CCKW-353	Truck, 2^1/$_2$ ton, oil servicing, 750 gallon, 6x6; F-3	1941	4,416cc	6
	CCKW-353	Truck, 2^1/$_2$ ton, shop, 6x6	1941	4,416cc	6

* V = cylinders in Vee formation; H = flat or horizontally-opposed configuration; (D) = diesel engine; (PG) = producer gas engine. * LWB = Long wheelbase.

Make	Model	Description	Date	Engine: capacity	cylinders*
GMC (cont)	CCKW-353	Truck, 2^1/$_2$ ton, stock rack, 6x6	1941	4,416cc	6
	CCKW-353	Truck, 2^1/$_2$ ton, van, 6x6; K-53, 60	1941	4,416cc	6
	CCKW-353	Truck, 2^1/$_2$ ton, van, high-lift, 6x6	1941	4,416cc	6
	CCKW-353	Truck, 2^1/$_2$ ton, water purification, 6x6	1941	4,416cc	6
	CCKW-353	Truck, 2^1/$_2$ ton, water, 700gallon, 6x6	1941	4,416cc	6
	CCX-453	Truck, 2^1/$_2$ ton, dump, 4x2	1941	4,416cc	6
	CCX-454	Truck, 2^1/$_2$ ton, stake/platform, 4x2	1941	4,416cc	6
	CCW-353	Truck, 2^1/$_2$ ton, cargo, 6x4	1941	4,416cc	6
	4929	Truck, 3 ton, cargo, 6x6	1938	3,769cc	6
	ACX-504	Truck, 3 ton, cargo, 4x2	1939	4,556cc	6
International	K6	Truck, 2^1/$_2$ ton, cargo, 4x2	1941	3,949cc	6
	K7	Truck, 2^1/$_2$ ton, cargo, 4x2	1941	4,408cc	6
	K7	Truck, 2^1/$_2$ ton, dump, 4x2	1941	4,408cc	6
	K7	Truck, 2^1/$_2$ ton, high-lift dump, 4x2	1942	4,408cc	6
	K7	Truck, 2^1/$_2$ ton, quarry dump, 4x2	1941	4,408cc	6
	K7	Truck, 2^1/$_2$ ton, stake/platform, LWB, 4x2	1941	4,408cc	6
	K7	Truck, 2^1/$_2$ ton, stake/platform, 4x2	1941	4,408cc	6
	M-5-6x4	Truck, 2^1/$_2$ ton, cargo, 6x4	1942	5,211cc	6
	M-5-6, M-5H-6	Truck, 2^1/$_2$ ton, cargo, 6x6	1941	5,211cc	6
	M-5-6, M-5H-6	Truck, 2^1/$_2$ ton, cargo, LWB, 6x6	1941	5,211cc	6
Linn	CFD	Truck, 2^1/$_2$ ton, tractor, 4x2	1941	n/a	n/a
Mack	EE, EF, EG	Truck, 2^1/$_2$ ton, cargo, 4x2	1940	4,752cc	6
	EE, EF, EG	Truck, 2^1/$_2$ ton, dump, 4x2	1940	4,752cc	6
	EE, EF, EG	Truck, 2^1/$_2$ ton, stake/platform, 4x2	1940	4,752cc	6
	EE, EF, EG	Truck, 2^1/$_2$ ton, tanker, 1,000 gallon, 4x2	1940	4,752cc	6
	EHS	Truck, 2^1/$_2$ ton, tanker, 1,000 gallon, 4x2	1940	5,080cc	6
	EHS	Truck, 2^1/$_2$ ton, water sprinkler, 4x2	1940	5,080cc	6
	EHUS	Truck, 2^1/$_2$ ton, van, 4x2	1940	5,080cc	6
	NB	Truck, 2^1/$_2$ ton, cargo, COE, 6x4	1940	4,146cc	6
	NB	Truck, 2^1/$_2$ ton, searchlight, COE, 6x4	1939	4,146cc	6
Reo	21-BHHS	Truck, 2^1/$_2$ ton, cargo, 4x2	1941	5,245cc	6
	21-XHHS	Truck, 2^1/$_2$ ton, dump, 4x2	1941	5,245cc	6
	US6-U3	Truck, 2^1/$_2$ ton, cargo, 6x6	1941	5,245cc	6
Studebaker	US6x4-U7, U8	Truck, 2^1/$_2$ ton, cargo, 6x4	1941	5,245cc	6
	US6x4-U6	Truck, 2^1/$_2$ ton, tractor, 6x4	1941	5,245cc	6
	US6- U2, U3	Truck, 2^1/$_2$ ton, cargo, 6x6	1941	5,245cc	6
	US6- U4	Truck, 2^1/$_2$ ton, dump, 6x6	1941	5,245cc	6
	US6-U5, U8	Truck, 2^1/$_2$ ton, tanker, 750 gallon; 6x6	1941	5,245cc	6
White	704S	Truck, 3 ton, cargo, 4x2	1939	4,425cc	6

* V = cylinders in Vee formation; H = flat or horizontally-opposed configuration; (D) = diesel engine; (PG) = producer gas engine. * LWB = Long wheelbase.

Heavy Trucks, over 3 tons

Make	Model	Description	Date	Engine: capacity	cylinders*
Germany					
Büssing-NAG	500A	Truck, heavy, cargo, 4x4	1940	7,412cc	6 (D)
	500S	Truck, heavy, cargo, 4x2	1940	7,412cc	6 (D)
	900A	Truck, heavy, cargo, 6x4	1937	13,540cc	6 (D)
	4500A-1	Truck, heavy, cargo, 4x4	1942	7,412cc	6 (D)
	4500S-1	Truck, heavy, cargo, 4x2	1942	7,412cc	6 (D)
Faun	L900D567	Truck, heavy, cargo, 6x4	1938	13,540cc	6 (D)
Henschel	6J2	Truck, heavy, cargo, 4x2	1937	n/a	6 (D)
KHD	GA145	Truck, heavy, cargo, 4x4	1940	7,412cc	6 (D)
	GS145	Truck, heavy, cargo, 4x2	1940	7,980cc	6 (D)
MAN	F2H6	Truck, heavy, cargo, 4x2	1935	7,412cc	6 (D)
	F4	Truck, 6½ ton, cargo, 4x2	1937	7,412cc	6 (D)
	ML4500A	Truck, heavy, cargo, 4x4	1940	7,412cc	6 (D)
	ML4500S	Truck, heavy, cargo, 4x2	1940	7,980cc	6 (D)
Mercedes-Benz	L3750	Truck, 4 ton, cargo, 4x2	1936	7,247cc	6 (D)
	LG4000	Truck, heavy, cargo, 6x6	1937	7,247cc	6 (D)
	LG65/3, 65/4	Truck, heavy, cargo, 8x8	1936	7,247cc	6 (D)
	L4500A	Truck, heavy, cargo, 4x4	1939	7,274cc	6 (D)
	L4500S	Truck, heavy, cargo, 4x2	1939	7,274cc	6 (D)
	L4500R	Truck, heavy, cargo, half-track	1943	7,274cc	6 (D)
ÖAF	ML4500A	Truck, heavy, cargo, 4x4 (Austrian)	1940	7,412cc	6 (D)
	ML4500S	Truck, heavy, cargo, 4x2 (Austrian)	1940	7,980cc	6 (D)
Renault	AGK	Truck, 5 ton, cargo, 4x2	1938	5,900cc	6
	AHR	Truck, 6 ton, cargo, 4x2	1941	5,900cc	6
Saurer	BT500	Truck, heavy, cargo, 4x2 (Swiss)	1944	7,274cc	6 (D)
Skoda	6ST6-T-H	Truck, 4 ton, cargo, 6x4 (Czech)	1939	8,280cc	6
	6ST6-T-HD	Truck, 4 ton, cargo, 6x4 (Czech)	1939	8,550cc	6 (D)
	6VD	Truck, 5 ton, cargo, 6x6 (Czech)	1937	8,550cc	6 (D)
	H	Truck, 4 ton, cargo, 6x4 (Czech)	1935	8,280cc	6
Tatra	T81	Truck, 6 ton, cargo, 6x4 (Czech)	1942	12,464cc	V8 (PG)
	T81H, HB	Truck, 6 ton, cargo, 6x4 (Czech)	1942	14,726cc	V8 (PG)
	T85	Truck, 5 ton, cargo, 6x4 (Czech)	1936	8,180cc	6
	T85A	Truck, 5 ton, cargo, 6x4 (Czech)	1939	8,180cc	6
	T111	Truck, 8 ton, cargo, 6x6 (Czech)	1943	14,825cc	V12 (D)
	T111R	Truck, 10 ton, cargo, 6x6 (Czech)	1943	14,825cc	V12 (D)
Great Britain					
AEC	Model 854	Truck, 10 ton, refueller, 2,000/2,500 gallon, 6x6	1939	7,413cc	6
	Model O854	Truck, 10 ton, refueller, 2,000/2,500 gallon, 6x6	1942	7,781cc	6 (D)
	Model O854	Truck, 10 ton, mobile oxygen plant, 6x6	1942	7,781cc	6 (D)
Albion	CX6N	Truck, 10 ton, GS, 6x4	1940	9,080cc	6 (D)
	CX23N	Truck, 10 ton, GS, 6x4	1941	9,080cc	6 (D)
Bedford	OWLD	Truck, 5 ton, flat platform, 4x2	1941	3,519cc	6
	OWLE	Truck, 5 ton, GS, 4x2	1941	3,519cc	6
	OWST	Truck, 5 ton, tipper, 4x2	1941	3,519cc	6
	OS	Truck, 6 ton, semi-trailer, GS, 4x2-2	1939	3,519cc	6
	OXC	Truck, 6 ton, semi-trailer, dropside, 4x2-2	1939	3,519cc	6

* V = cylinders in Vee formation; H = flat or horizontally-opposed configuration; (D) = diesel engine; (PG) = producer gas engine.

Make	Model	Description	Date	Engine: capacity	cylinders*
Bedford	OXC	Truck, 6 ton, semi-trailer, flat platform, 4x2-2	1939	3,519cc	6
(cont)	OXC	Truck, 6 ton, semi-trailer, GS, 4x2-2	1939	3,519cc	6
	OXC	Truck, 6 ton, semi-trailer, low-loading, 4x2-2	1939	3,519cc	6
	OXC	Truck, 6 ton, semi-trailer, petrol, 1,200 gallon, 4x2-2	1939	3,519cc	6
	OXC	Truck, 6 ton, semi-trailer, petrol, 2,000 gallon, 4x2-2	1939	3,519cc	6
	OXC	Truck, 6 ton, semi-trailer, torpedo, 4x2-2	1939	3,519cc	6
	QLC	Truck, 6 ton, semi-trailer, GS, 4x4-2	1941	3,519cc	6
Commer	Q6	Truck, 6 ton, GS, 4x2	1939	4,080cc	6
Dennis	Pax D Mk II	Truck, 5 ton, cesspool emptier, 750 gallon, 4x2	1944	6,502cc	4 (D)
	Max Mk I	Truck, 6 ton, GS, 4x2	1940	6,502cc	4 (D)
	Max Mk II	Truck, 6 ton, GS, 4x2	1943	6,502cc	4 (D)
ERF	2CI4	Truck, 6 ton, GS, 4x2	1939	5,541cc	4 (D)
Foden	DG4/6	Truck, 6 ton, GS, 4x2	1940	5,541cc	4 (D)
	DG6/10	Truck, 10 ton, GS, 6x4	1939	8,369cc	6 (D)
	DG6/12	Truck, 10 ton, auto processing, 6x4	1941	8,369cc	6 (D)
	DG6/12	Truck, 10 ton, enlarging and rectifying, 6x4	1941	8,369cc	6 (D)
	DG6/12	Truck, 10 ton, GS, 6x4	1941	8,369cc	6 (D)
	DG6/12	Truck, 10 ton, photo mechanical, 6x4	1941	8,369cc	6 (D)
	DG6/12	Truck, 10 ton, printing, 6x4	1941	8,369cc	6 (D)
Ford	Thames 7V	Truck, 4-6 ton, tipper, 4x2	1940	3,621cc	V8
Leyland	Badger	Truck, 6 ton, GS, 4x2	1932	n/a	4
	Hippo Mk I	Truck, 10 ton, GS, 6x4	1939	8,990cc	6 (D)
	Hippo Mk II, IIB	Truck, 10 ton, GS, 6x4	1944	7,399cc	6 (D)
Maudslay	Militant	Truck, 6 ton, GS, 4x2	1940	5,541cc	4 (D)

Italy

Make	Model	Description	Date	Engine: capacity	cylinders*
Alfa Romeo	800RE	Truck, heavy, cargo, 4x2	1940	8,725cc	6 (D)
	800RE	Truck, heavy, cargo, half-track	1940	8,725cc	6 (D)
Breda	51	Truck, heavy, cargo, 6x4	1941	8,850cc	6 (D)
	52	Truck, heavy, cargo, 6x4	1942	8,850cc	6 (D)
Ceirano	50CMA/75CK	Truck, heavy, cargo, 4x2; and others	1933	5,570cc	4
Fiat	633NM	Truck, heavy, cargo, 4x2	1935	5,570cc	4 (D)
	633BM, GM	Truck, heavy, cargo, 4x2	1936	6,647cc	4
	665NL	Truck, heavy, cargo, 4x2	1942	6,647cc	6 (D)
	665NM	Truck, heavy, cargo, 4x2	1942	9,365cc	6 (D)
	634N	Truck, 7½ ton, water tanker, 4x2	1933	8,355cc	6
SPA	Dovunque 41	Truck, 5-6 ton, cargo, 6x6	1943	9,365cc	6
Isotta-Fraschini	D80MO	Truck, heavy, cargo, 4x2	1935	7,273cc	6 (D)
	D80COM	Truck, heavy, cargo, 4x2	1939	7,273cc	6 (D)
Lancia	RO MNP-264	Truck, heavy, van, 4x2	1934	3,180cc	H2 (D)
	3RO N 'Mil' 564	Truck, heavy, cargo, 4x2	1938	6,875cc	5
OM	3BOD 'Mil'	Truck, heavy, cargo, 4x2	1938	5,702cc	4 (D)
	Ursus	Truck, heavy, cargo, 4x2	1939	7,980cc	6 (D)

Japan

Make	Model	Description	Date	Engine: capacity	cylinders*
Isuzu	TB60 Type 2	Truck, 7 ton, cargo, 4x2	1941	8,550cc	6 (D)
	TH10	Truck, 20 ton, dump, 6x4	1943	8,553cc	6 (D)

* V = cylinders in Vee formation; H = flat or horizontally-opposed configuration; (D) = diesel engine; (PG) = producer gas engine.

Make	Model	Description	Date	Engine: capacity	cylinders*
Soviet Union					
YaAZ	10	Truck, 8 ton, cargo, 6x4; and AA gun	1932	7,020cc	6
	12	Truck, 12 ton, cargo, 8x8	1932	7,020cc	6
United States of America					
Autocar	C7066	Truck, 4 ton, cargo, 6x6	1940	7,391cc	6
	U7144-T	Truck, 4-5 ton, tractor, COE, 4x4	1941	8,669cc	6
	C50	Truck, 5 ton, dump, 4x2	1941	7,391cc	6
	C50	Truck, 5 ton, stake/platform, 4x2	1941	7,391cc	6
	C70	Truck, 5 ton, cargo, 4x2	1940	5,244cc	6
	C70-T	Truck, 5 ton, tractor, 4x2	1943	5,244cc	6
	C7064	Truck, 5 ton, cargo, 6x4	1940	7,391cc	6
	U5044	Truck, 5 ton, tractor, COE, 4x4	1941	5,244cc	6
	U70	Truck, 5 ton, fuel/oil servicing, 1,600 gallon, 4x2	1937	5,244cc	6
	U8144-T	Truck, 5-6 ton, tractor, 4x4	1944	8,669cc	6
	U8144-T	Truck, 5-6 ton, pontoon tractor, 4x4	1941	8,669cc	6
	U8144	Truck, 5-6 ton, dump, 4x4	1942	8,669cc	6
	U8144	Truck, 5-6 ton, radio, 4x4	1941	8,669cc	6
	U8144	Truck, 5-6 ton, van, 4x4	1941	8,669cc	6
	C9064	Truck, 10 ton, tractor, 6x4	1940	8,669cc	6
Biederman	C-2, F-1, P-1	Truck, 7$\frac{1}{2}$ ton, tractor, 6x6	1942	14,011cc	6
Brockway	B146S	Truck, 4 ton, fuel, 833 gallon, 4x2	1940	5,400cc	6
	B156	Truck, 10 ton, tractor, 4x2	1940	6,600cc	6
	B166S	Truck, 6 ton, fuel, 1,660 gallon, 4x2	1940	6,600cc	6
	B666	Truck, 6 ton, bridge erection, 6x6	1942	14,011cc	6
Cook Bros	T20	Truck, 8 ton, cargo, 8x8	1944	9,865cc	6
Corbitt	-	Truck, 6 ton, cargo, 6x6	1939	12,766cc	6
	50SD6	Truck, 6 ton, tractor, 6x6	1941	14,011cc	6
	40SD6	Truck, 8 ton, tractor, 6x4	1942	12,946cc	6
	50SD4	Truck, 10 ton, tractor, 6x4	1942	12,946cc	6
Dart	200-353	Truck, 10 ton, tanker, 3,300 gallon, 6x4	1941	8,472cc	6
Diamond T	Model 967	Truck, 4 ton, cargo, 6x6	1941	8,210cc	6
	Model 968, 968A	Truck, 4 ton, bituminous supply, 800 gallon, 6x6	1941	8,669cc	6
	Model 968, 968A	Truck, 4 ton, cargo, 6x6	1941	8,669cc	6
	Model 968, 968A	Truck, 4 ton, water distributor, 1,000 gallon, 6x6	1941	8,669cc	6
	Model 970, 970A	Truck, 4 ton, cargo, 6x6	1941	8,669cc	6
	Model 970, 970A	Truck, 4 ton, map reproduction, 6x6	1941	8,669cc	6
	Model 970, 970A	Truck, 4 ton, pontoon, 6x6	1941	8,669cc	6
	Model 972	Truck, 4 ton, dump, 6x6	1943	8,669cc	6
	Model 975, 975A	Truck, 4 ton, folding boat equipment, 6x6	1942	8,669cc	6
	Model 975, 975A	Truck, 4 ton, GS, 6x6	1942	8,669cc	6
	Model 975, 975A	Truck, 4 ton, machinery, 6x6, (various)	1942	8,669cc	6
	Model 975, 975A	Truck, 4 ton, pontoon, 6x6	1942	8,669cc	6
	Model 806	Truck, 5 ton, ammunition, 4x2	1940	8,669cc	6
	Model 806	Truck, 5 ton, refrigerator, 4x2	1940	8,669cc	6
Federal	29K	Truck, 3$\frac{1}{2}$ ton, cargo, 4x2	1941	8,669cc	6
	29K	Truck, 3$\frac{1}{2}$ ton, tractor, 4x2	1941	8,669cc	6

* V = cylinders in Vee formation; H = flat or horizontally-opposed configuration; (D) = diesel engine; (PG) = producer gas engine.

Make	Model	Description	Date	Engine: capacity	cylinders*
Federal	94x43A	Truck, 4-5 ton, dump, COE, 4x4	1941	8,669cc	6
(cont)	94x43A, B, C	Truck, 4-5 ton, tractor, COE, 4x4	1941	8,669cc	6
	55L	Truck, 5 ton, cargo, 4x2	1941	8,669cc	6
	55L	Truck, 5 ton, dump, 4x2	1941	8,669cc	6
	55L	Truck, 5 ton, stake/platform, 4x2	1941	8,669cc	6
	605	Truck, 7½ ton, tractor, 6x6	1942	14,011cc	6
	606	Truck, 7½ ton, tractor, 6x6	1942	14,011cc	6
	604	Truck, 10 ton, cargo, 6x4	1942	11,012cc	6 (D)
	604	Truck, 10 ton, tractor, 6x4	1942	11,012cc	6 (D)
Ford/E&L Transport	-	Truck, tractor, 6x4	1942	7,834cc	2x V8
FWD	HAR-1	Truck, 4 ton, cargo, 4x4	1942	5,244cc	6
	HAR-03	Tractor, 4 ton, 4x4, with 6 ton semi-trailer, GS	1942	5,244cc	6
	HST	Truck, 5-6 ton, utility line, COE, 4x4	1940	5,244cc	6
	SU	Truck, 5-6 ton, cargo, COE, 4x4	1944	8,472cc	6
	CU	Truck, 16 ton, tractor, 4x4	1942	8,472cc	6
	YU	Truck, 6 ton, pontoon bridge erection, 4x4	1941	8,603cc	6
	H	Truck, 10 ton, workshop, 4x4	1944	6,620cc	6
GMC	AFKX-804-8F	Truck, 4 ton, shop van, 4x4	1941	6,981cc	6
	AC-625	Truck, 5 ton, stake/platform, 4x2	1945	5,912cc	6
	AC-723	Truck, 5 ton, dump, 4x2	1940	6,981cc	6
	AC-725	Truck, 5 ton, stake/platform, 4x2	1940	6,981cc	6
	AC-803	Truck, 5 ton, dump, 4x2	1940	6,981cc	6
	AC-805	Truck, 5 ton, stake/platform, 4x2	1941	6,981cc	6
	AFX-803	Truck, 5 ton, fuel servicing, 1,200 gallon, 4x2	1941	6,981cc	6
	CCW-353	Truck, 5 ton, cargo, 6x4	1942	6,981cc	6
	CCW-353	Truck, 5 ton, dump, 6x4	1942	6,981cc	6
	ACW-853	Truck, 8 ton, tractor, 6x4	1941	6,981cc	6
Hug	50-6	Truck, 7½ ton, cargo, 6x6	1940	12,946cc	6
International	D60	Truck, 5 ton, tractor, 4x2	1937	5,735cc	6
	K8	Truck, 5 ton, cargo, 4x2	1940	7,391cc	6
	KR8	Truck, 5 ton, tractor, 4x2	1940	7,391cc	6
	KR8R	Truck, 5 ton, tractor, 4x2	1942	4,146cc	6
	KR11	Truck, 5 ton, cargo, 4x2	1941	7,391cc	6
	KR11	Truck, 5 ton, dump, 4x2	1941	7,391cc	6
	KR11	Truck, 5 ton, fuel servicing, 1,200 gallon, 4x2	1944	7,391cc	6
	KR11	Truck, 5 ton, high-lift dump, 4x2	1942	7,391cc	6
	KR11	Truck, 5 ton, tractor, 4x2	1944	7,391cc	6
	IH-542-9	Truck, 5 ton, tractor, COE, 4x2; M425	1944	7,391cc	6
	IH-542-11	Truck, 5 ton, tractor, COE, 4x2; M426	1944	7,391cc	6
	KR10	Truck, 6 ton, GS, 4x2	1940	5,899cc	6
	KR10	Truck, 6 ton, tractor, 4x2	1941	5,899cc	6
	KR11	Truck, 7 ton, GS, 4x2	1940	5,899cc	6
	K8F	Truck, 8 ton, cargo, 6x4	1940	7,391cc	6
	IH-542-9 mod	Truck, 10 ton, cargo, COE, 6x4	1944	7,391cc	6
	IH-542-9 mod	Truck, 10 ton, cargo, COE, 4x2	1944	7,391cc	6
Kenworth	-	Truck, 5 ton, dump, 6x6	1943	8,226cc	6
	-	Truck, 5 ton, tractor, 4x2	1944	8,226cc	6

* V = cylinders in Vee formation; H = flat or horizontally-opposed configuration; (D) = diesel engine; (PG) = producer gas engine.

Make	Model	Description	Date	Engine: capacity	cylinders*
Mack	EH	Truck, 5 ton, cargo, 4x2	1943	5,080cc	6
	EH	Truck, 5 ton, fuel and oil servicing, 4x2	1937	5,080cc	6
	EHT	Truck, 5 ton, tractor, 4x2	1943	5,801cc	6
	EHU	Truck, 5 ton, cargo, COE, 4x2	1942	5,080cc	6
	EHUT	Truck, 5 ton, tractor, COE, 4x2	1942	5,801cc	6
	FPD	Truck, 5 ton, dump, 4x2	1940	7,669cc	6 (D)
	NJU1	Truck, 5-6 ton, pontoon tractor, 4x4	1940	8,718cc	6
	NJU2	Truck, 5-6 ton, topographical tractor, 4x4	1941	8,718cc	6
	NM1, NM2	Truck, 6 ton, cargo, 6x6	1940	11,586cc	6
	NM3	Truck, 6 ton, cargo, 6x6	1941	11,586cc	6
	NM4, NM5	Truck, 6 ton, cargo, 6x6	1942	11,586cc	6
	NM7, NM8	Truck, 6 ton, cargo, 6x6	1944	11,586cc	6
	NM8 mod	Truck, 10 ton, cargo, 6x6	1944	11,586cc	6
	FG	Truck, 10 ton, dump, 4x2	1942	7,669cc	6
	NR1	Truck, 10 ton, cargo, 6x4	1940	8,505cc	6 (D)
	NR2, NR3, NR5	Truck, 10 ton, cargo, 6x4	1941	8,505cc	6 (D)
	NR6, NR7, NR8	Truck, 10 ton, cargo, 6x4	1942	8,505cc	6 (D)
	NR9-NR13	Truck, 10 ton, cargo, 6x4	1943	8,505cc	6 (D)
	LFT	Truck, 12 ton, tractor, 4x2	1942	7,063cc	6
	FCSW	Truck, 30 ton, dump, 6x4	1941	11,586cc	6
Marmon-Herrington	U7144-T	Truck, 4-5 ton, tractor, COE, 4x4	1941	8,669cc	6
	H-542-9	Truck, 5 ton, tractor, COE, 4x2; M425	1944	7,391cc	6
	H-542-11	Truck, 5 ton, tractor, COE, 4x2; M426	1944	7,391cc	6
Oshkosh	TR	Truck, 15 ton, tractor, 4x4	1940	n/a	n/a
Reo	23BHRS	Truck, 5 ton, dump, 4x2	1941	14,011cc	6
	23XHHRS	Truck, 5 ton, cargo, 4x2	1941	14,011cc	6
	27XFS, 29XFS	Truck, 7$\frac{1}{2}$ ton, tractor, 6x6	1942	14,011cc	6
	28XS	Truck, 10 ton, tractor, 6x4	1944	11,012cc	6 (D)
Studebaker	K30	Truck, 5 ton, cargo, 4x2	1939	n/a	6
Ward LaFrance	106	Truck, 4 ton, cargo, 6x6	1940	8,226cc	6
	-	Truck, 5 ton, tractor, 4x2	1944	8,226cc	6
	204	Truck, 10 ton, tractor, 6x4	1940	8,226cc	6
White	950X6	Truck, 4 ton, cargo, 6x6	1939	5,932cc	6
	444T	Truck, 4-5 ton, tractor, COE, 4x4	1941	8,669cc	6
	666	Truck, 6 ton, cargo, 6x6; and others	1941	14,011cc	6
	760	Truck, 10 ton, cargo, 4x2	1940	5,932cc	6
	1064	Truck, 10 ton, cargo, 6x4	1942	11,012cc	6 (D)

* V = cylinders in Vee formation; H = flat or horizontally-opposed configuration; (D) = diesel engine; (PG) = producer gas engine.

Above: A column of Red Army S-2 fully-tracked vehicles on the Eastern Front during the battle for Moscow, 8 December 1941. *(PW)*

Right: An Italian Army Lancia 4x4 medium truck loaded with troops in the North African desert, 1 July 1942. *(UB)*

Tractors and Prime Movers

Make	Model	Description	Date	Engine: capacity	cylinders*
Australia					
Chevrolet	CGT	Tractor, artillery, 4x4	1940	3,540cc	6
Ford	01T/MH	Tractor, artillery, 4x4	1940	3,622cc	V8
	F60L C298QF	Truck, 3 ton, Bofors SP, 4x4	1940	3,917cc	V8
Canada					
Chevrolet	CGT 8440	Tractor, field artillery, 4x4	1940	3,540cc	6
	CGT 8440	Truck, 30cwt, anti-tank portee and fire (2 pounder), 4x4	1940	3,540cc	6
	C60L 8443	Truck, 3 ton, anti-tank portee and fire, 4x4	1940	3,540cc	6
Ford	FGT C291Q	Tractor, field artillery, 4x4	1940	3,917cc	V8
	F60B C39QB	Truck, 3 ton, Bofors SP, 4x4	1944	3,917cc	V8
	F60L C298QF	Truck, 3 ton, anti-tank portee and fire, 4x4	1940	3,917cc	V8
	F60S C01QF	Truck, 3 ton, Bofors SP, 4x4	1940	3,917cc	V8
Germany					
Adler	D7	Tractor, light, 1 ton, semi-track; SdKfz10	1934	4,170cc	6
	HL kl 6	Tractor, light, 3 ton, semi-track; SdKfz11	1938	4,170cc	6
Borgward	HL kl 6	Tractor, light, 3 ton, semi-track; SdKfz11	1938	4,170cc	6
Bussing-NAG	D7	Tractor, light, 1 ton, semi-track; SdKfz10	1934	4,170cc	6
	BN9, BN17	Tractor, medium, 5 ton, semi-track; SdKfz6	1934	3,790cc	6
	BN m 8	Tractor, medium, 8 ton, semi-track; SdKfz7	1934	6,191cc	6
	sWS	Tractor, heavy, semi-track	1943	4,198cc	6
	900A	Truck, heavy, tank carrier, 6x4	1937	13,540cc	6 (D)
Demag	D7	Tractor, light, 1 ton, semi-track; SdKfz10	1934	4,170cc	6
Famo	F2, F3	Tractor, heavy, 18 ton, semi-track; SdKfz9	1939	10,838cc	V12
Faun	L900D567	Truck, heavy, tank carrier, 6x4	1938	13,540cc	6 (D)
	ZR	Tractor, heavy, 4x2	1939	13,540cc	6 (D)
Hanomag	HL kl 6	Tractor, light, 3 ton, semi-track; SdKfz11	1938	4,170cc	6
	SS55	Tractor, heavy, 4x2	1939	5,195cc	4 (D)
	SS100	Tractor, heavy, 4x2	1936	8,553cc	6 (D)
Hansa Lloyd	HL m 11	Tractor, medium, 8 ton, semi-track; SdKfz7	1934	6,191cc	6
Kaelble	Z2S	Tractor, medium, 4x2	1936	4,908cc	2 (D)
	Z6V2A	Tractor, heavy, 6x4	1938	13,253cc	6 (D)
	Z6WA	Tractor, heavy, 4x2	1935	13,253cc	6 (D)
KHD	RSO/3	Tractor, full track	1944	5,322cc	4 (D)
Krauss-Maffei	KM m 8-11	Tractor, medium, 8 ton, semi-track; SdKfz7	1939	6,191cc	6
	KM s 8-10	Tractor, heavy, 12 ton, semi-track; SdKfz8	1936	7,973cc	V12
Krupp	L2H43	Truck, light, artillery tractor, 6x4	1934	3,308cc	4
	L2H143	Truck, light, artillery tractor, 6x4	1937	3,308cc	4
Laffly	S35T	Tractor, artillery, 6x6 (French)	1935	6,232cc	6
Latil	FTARH 'Ostfront'	Tractor, wheeled, heavy, 4x4 (French)	1943	6,040cc	4
Mercedes-Benz	DB9, DB17	Tractor, medium, 5 ton, semi-track; SdKfz6	1934	3,790cc	6
	DB m 8	Tractor, medium, 8 ton, semi-track; SdKfz7	1934	6,191cc	6
	DB s 8-10	Tractor, heavy, 12 ton, semi-track; SdKfz8	1936	7,973cc	V12
MWC	D7	Tractor, light, 1 ton, semi-track; SdKfz.10	1934	4,170cc	6
NSU	HK-101	Tractor, motorcycle, semi-track (Kettenkrad); SdKfz2	1940	1,478cc	4

* V = cylinders in Vee formation; H = flat or horizontally-opposed configuration; (D) = diesel engine; (PG) = producer gas engine.

Right: Diamond T Model 980/981 prime mover with the 45-ton Rogers trailer decked over to carry dense stores. A number of these vehicles were used in this way during the Red Ball Express operation. *(TM)*

Make	Model	Description	Date	Engine: capacity	cylinders*
Praga	T6-SS	Tractor, artillery, full track (Czech)	1944	7,754cc	6
	BN9, BN17	Tractor, medium, 5 ton, semi-track; SdKfz6	1934	3,790cc	6
Saurer	D7	Tractor, light, 1 ton, semi-track; SdKfz10	1934	4,170cc	6
Skoda	-	Tractor, heavy, 12 ton, semi-track; SdKfz8	1936	7,973cc	V12
	175 RSO	Tractor, heavy, wheeled, 4x4 (Czech)	1942	6,024cc	4 (D)
	6K	Truck, 11 ton, tank carrier, 4x4 (Czech)	1936	12,920cc	6
Somua	MCG	Tractor, artillery, half-track (French)	1936	4,712cc	4
	MCL5	Tractor, artillery, half-track (French)	1936	6,232cc	4
Steyr-Puch	470 RSO/01	Truck, 1½ ton, prime mover, full track (Austrian)	1942	3,517cc	V8
Unic	P107	Tractor, artillery, half-track (French)	1937	3,450cc	4
	TU1	Tractor, artillery, half-track (French)	1940	2,150cc	4
Tatra	SWS	Tractor, heavy, semi-track (Czech)	1943	4,198cc	6
Great Britain					
AEC	Matador 853	Tractor, medium artillery, 4x4	1937	7,413cc	6
	Matador O853	Tractor, medium artillery, 4x4	1938	7,781cc	6 (D)
	850 (R6T)	Tractor, artillery, 6x6	1936	6,126cc	6
Albion	CX22S	Tractor, heavy artillery, 6x4	1943	9,080cc	6 (D)
	CX24S	Transporter, 20 ton (later 15 ton), 6x4-8	1942	10,487cc	6
	FT15N	Tractor, field artillery, 6x6	1944	4,566cc	6
Austin	K5	Truck, anti-tank portee and fire (6-pounder), 4x4	1941	3,995cc	6
Bedford	MWG	Truck, 15cwt, anti-tank portee, 4x2	1936	3,519cc	6
	MWT	Truck, 15cwt, anti-tank tractor, 4x2	1936	3,519cc	6
	OXC	Truck, 3 ton, tractor, semi-trailer, 4x2-2	1939	3,519cc	6
	QLC	Truck, anti-tank portee and fire (6-pounder), 4x4	1941	3,519cc	6
	QLB	Tractor, light anti-aircraft (Bofors), 3 ton, GS, 4x4	1941	3,519cc	6

* V = cylinders in Vee formation; H = flat or horizontally-opposed configuration; (D) = diesel engine; (PG) = producer gas engine.

Make	Model	Description	Date	Engine: capacity	cylinders*
Crossley/Tasker	-	Truck, 5 ton, low loader, 4x4-2	n/a	n/a	4
David Brown	AC1	Tractor, full track	1940	2,523cc	4
	AW500, VIG1/100	Tractor, aircraft, 4x2	1941	2,523cc	4
	VIG1/462	Tractor, aircraft, 4x2	1943	2,523cc	4
Ford-Roadless	N	Tractor, full track	1936	4,380cc	4
	N	Tractor, half track	1938	4,380cc	4
Ford-Tructor	WOT3	Tractor, 30cwt, GS, 4x2	1939	3,621cc	V8
Guy	Quad Ant	Tractor, field artillery, 4x4	1939	3,519cc	6
Karrier	KT4 Spider	Tractor, field artillery, 4x4	1939	4,086cc	6
Morris-Commercial	C8/FAT	Tractor, field artillery, 4x4	1938	3,686cc	4
	C8/AT	Tractor, anti-tank (17-pounder), 4x4	1938	3,519cc	4
	C8/MG	Truck, anti-tank portee (2-pounder), 4x4	1938	3,519cc	4
	C8/P	Tractor, anti-tank (17-pounder), 4x4	1938	3,519cc	4
	C9/B	Carrier, SP, 40mm AA (Bofors), 4x4	1938	3,519cc	4
	CS8	Truck, 15cwt, anti-tank tractor, 4x2	1938	3,519cc	6
	CD/SW	Tractor, light anti-aircraft (Bofors), 6x4	1938	3,519cc	6
Scammell	MH6	Tractor, GS, 3x2	1933	2,043cc	4
	Pioneer R100	Tractor, heavy artillery, 6x4	1938	8,369cc	6 (D)
	Pioneer TRMU/20	Tractor-trailer, tank transporter, 20 ton, 6x4-8	1937	8,369cc	6 (D)
	Pioneer TRMU/30	Tractor-trailer, tank transporter/recovery 30 ton, 6x4-8	1939	8,369cc	6 (D)

Italy

Make	Model	Description	Date	Engine: capacity	cylinders*
Breda	32	Tractor, heavy, artillery, 4x4	1932	8,142cc	4
	33	Tractor, heavy, engineers, 4x4	1933	8,142cc	4
	51	Truck, heavy, mobile gun mount, 6x4	1941	8,850cc	6 (D)
	61	Tractor, medium, 8 ton, semi-track	1943	7,412cc	6
Ceirano	50CMA/75CK	Truck, heavy, anti-aircraft gun, 4x2	1933	4,714cc	4
Fiat	SC727	Tractor, artillery, semi-track	1943	5,750cc	6
	621PN	Truck, medium, gun portee, 6x4	1934	4,580cc	4 (D)
OCI	708CM	Tractor, artillery, full-track	1935	2,520cc	4
Pavesi	P4/100	Tractor, heavy, artillery, 4x4	1936	4,724cc	4
Savigliano	OS88	Tractor, artillery, full-track	1943	6,875cc	5 (D)
SPA	Dovunque 41	Tractor, heavy, artillery, 6x6	1943	9,365cc	6 (D)
	TL37	Tractor, light, artillery, 4x4	1937	4,053cc	4
	TM40	Tractor, medium, 4x4	1941	9,365cc	6 (D)

Japan

Make	Model	Description	Date	Engine: capacity	cylinders*
Isuzu	Type 94A	Truck, 1½ ton, prime mover, 6x4	1934	4,390cc	6
	Type 94B	Truck, 1½ ton, prime mover, 6x4	1934	4,840cc	4 (D)
	Type 96A	Truck, 1½ ton, prime mover, 6x4	1937	4,390cc	6
	Type 96B	Truck, 1 ½ ton, prime mover, 6x4	1937	4,840cc	4 (D)
	-	Tractor, 6 ton, artillery, half-track; Type 98	1938	10,850cc	6 (D)
	Ro-Ke	Tractor, 6 ton, artillery, full-track; Type 98	1937	8,553cc	6 (D)
	TU10	Truck, 3 ton, machine gun carrier, 6x4; Type 94A	1934	4,390cc	6
	TU10	Truck, 3 ton, gun prime mover, 6x4; Type 96A	1934	4,390cc	6
	TU23	Truck, 3 ton, gun prime mover, 6x4; Type 96B	1941	5,100cc	6

* V = cylinders in Vee formation; H = flat or horizontally-opposed configuration; (D) = diesel engine; (PG) = producer gas engine.

Right: Although primarily designed as a tank transporter, the Diamond T Model 980/981 was what, these days, we would call a heavy equipment transporter... in this case, the load is an Allis-Chalmers high-speed artillery tractor. The curved structure over the ballast box is temporary living quarters for the crew. *(PW)*

Make	Model	Description	Date	Engine: capacity	cylinders*
KATO	-	Tractor, general purpose, 4x2	n/a	n/a	4
	Yo-Ke	Tractor, 4 ton, artillery, full-track; Type 94	1934	n/a	V8
Kokura or Sagami	Ko-Hi	Tractor, 5 ton, half-track; Type 98	1938	10,850cc	6 (D)
	Shi-Ke	Tractor, 4 ton, artillery, full-track; Type 98	1938	6,362cc	V8
	I-Ke	Tractor, 5 ton, artillery, full-track; Type 92A	1931	n/a	6
	I-Ke	Tractor, 5 ton, artillery, full-track; Type 92B	1932	n/a	6 (D)
	Ni-Ku	Tractor, 8 ton, artillery, full-track; Type 92A	1932	n/a	6
	Ni-Ku	Tractor, 8 ton, artillery, full-track; Type 92B	1938	n/a	6 (D)
	Ho-Fu	Tractor, 13 ton, artillery, full-track; Type 95A	1935	n/a	V8
	Ho-Fu	Tractor, 13 ton, artillery, full-track; Type 95B	1938	14,470cc	V8 (D)
		Tractor, medium artillery, full-track	n/a	14,470cc	V8 (D)
	Chi-Ke	KeTractor, heavy artillery, full-track	n/a	21,703cc	V12 (D)
Komatsu	81	Tractor, 3 ton, full-tracked	n/a	n/a	4
Soviet Union					
ChTZ	Stalinets S-2	Tractor, artillery, full-track	1939	13,520cc	4 (D)
	Stalinets S-60	Tractor, artillery, full-track	1932	11,282cc	4 (D)
	Stalinets S-65	Tractor, artillery, full-track	1937	18,540cc	4 (D)
	Stalinets SG-65	Tractor, artillery, full-track	1937	18,540cc	4 (PG)
STZ	3	Tractor, light, prime mover, full-track	1937	7,460cc	4
	5	Tractor, light, prime mover, full-track	1938	7,460cc	4
	Voroshilovets	Tractor, heavy, prime mover, full-track	1939	38,880cc	V12 (D)
KhPZ	AT-45	Tractor, heavy, prime mover, full-track	1944	38,880cc	V12 (D)
	Komintern	Tractor, medium, prime mover, full-track	1934	15,095cc	4
	Komsomolets T-20	Tractor, light, prime mover, full-track	1936	3,285cc	4
	Voroshilovets	Tractor, heavy, prime mover, full-track	1939	38,880cc	V12 (D)
YaAz	Yaroslavl 12	Tractor, light, artillery, full-track	1943	4,654cc	4 (D)
	Yaroslavl 13F	Tractor, light, artillery, full-track	1943	5,522cc	4

* V = cylinders in Vee formation; H = flat or horizontally-opposed configuration; (D) = diesel engine; (PG) = producer gas engine.

Make	Model	Description	Date	Engine: capacity	cylinders*
United States of America					
Allis-Chalmers	-	Snow tractor, half-track; M7	1943	2,199cc	4
	-	Tractor, 18 ton, high speed; M4, M4A1	1943	13,388cc	6
	HD7W	Tractor, medium, full-track; M1	1940	3,490cc	4 (D)
	-	Tractor, 38 ton, high speed; M6	1943	26,776cc	6
	HD10W	Tractor, heavy, full-track; M1	1940	4,654cc	4 (D)
Caterpillar	D4-4G	Tractor, light, full-track; M2	1938	5,735cc	4 (D)
	D6-4R, 5R	Tractor, medium, full-track; M1	1941	7,669cc	6 (D)
	D7-7M	Tractor, heavy, full-track	1940	13,618cc	4 (D)
	D8-2U	Tractor, heavy, full-track	1940	20,418cc	6 (D)
Cleveland Tractor	MG1, MG2	Tractor, 7 ton, high speed; M2	1941	6,620cc	6
Dart	-	Truck-trailer, 40 ton, tank transporter, 6x6-4; T3	1942	28,463cc	6
Diamond T	Model 967	Truck, 4 ton, cargo/prime mover, 6x6	1941	8,210cc	6
	Model 968A	Truck, 4 ton, cargo/prime mover, 6x6	1941	8,669cc	6
	Model 970A	Truck, 4 ton, cargo/prime mover, 6x6	1941	8,669cc	6
	Model 980/981	Truck, 12 ton, prime mover, 6x4; M20	1941	14,500cc	6 (D)
	Model 980/981	Transporter, 30 ton, semi-trailer recovery, 6x4-8	1942	14,500cc	6 (D)
Dodge	T214	Carriage, motor, 37mm gun; M4, M6; WC55	1941	3,772cc	6
FWD	CU	Truck, 5-6 ton, tractor, timber haulage, COE, 4x4	1942	6,178cc	6 (D)
	SU Special	Truck, 5-6 ton, prime mover, COE, 4x4	1944	8,472cc	6
	SU Special	Truck, medium artillery, COE, 4x4	1944	8,472cc	6
GMC	4929	Truck, 3 ton, prime mover, 6x6	1938	3,769cc	6
International	TD9	Tractor, light, full-track; M2	1940	5,481cc	4 (D)
	K8F	Truck, 8 ton, prime mover, 6x4	1940	7,391cc	6
	TD14	Tractor, medium, full-track; M1	1940	7,550cc	6 (D)
	-	Tractor, medium, full-track; M5	n/a	9,373cc	6
	-	Tractor, 13 ton, high speed; M5, M5A1, M5A2	1943	9,373cc	6
	TD18	Tractor, heavy, full-track; M1	1940	5,481cc	4 (D)
Iron Fireman	-	Snow tractor; T36	1944	3,772cc	6
Mack	EXBX, EXBX-2	Truck, 18 ton, tank transporter, 6x4	1940	8,505cc	6
	NM1, NM2	Truck, 6 ton, cargo/prime mover, 6x6	1940	11,586cc	6
	NM3	Truck, 6 ton, cargo/prime mover, 6x6	1941	11,586cc	6
	NM4, NM5	Truck, 6 ton, cargo/prime mover, 6x6	1942	11,586cc	6
	NM7, NM8	Truck, 6 ton, cargo/prime mover, 6x6	1944	11,586cc	6
	NO1	Truck, 7½ ton, prime mover, 6x6	1941	11,586cc	6
	NO2, 3, 6, 7	Truck, 7½ ton, prime mover, 6x6	1943	11,586cc	6
	NQ	Truck, 7½ ton, prime mover, 6x6	1942	11,586cc	6
	NR4	Truck, 13 ton, tank transporter, 6x4	1941	8,505cc	6
Minneapolis-Moline	NTX	Truck, 1½ ton, prime mover, 4x4	1942	3,384cc	4
	GTX	Truck, 7½ ton, prime mover, 6x6	1940	9,911cc	6
Pacific	TR1	Truck-trailer, 45 ton, tank transporter, 6x6-4; M25	1943	17,862cc	6
White	666	Truck, 6 ton, prime mover, 6x6	1941	14,011cc	6
	920	Truck, 18 ton, tank transporter, 6x4	1940	8,670cc	6
White-Ruxtall	922	Truck, 18 ton, tank transporter, 6x4	1940	8,670cc	6

* V = cylinders in Vee formation; H = flat or horizontally-opposed configuration; (D) = diesel engine; (PG) = producer gas engine.

Wreckers and Recovery Vehicles

Make	Model	Description	Date	Engine: capacity	cylinders*
Australia					
Ford	296T	Truck, 3 ton, breakdown gantry, number 3A, 6x6	1942	3,622cc	V8
Ford-Marmon	11T/MH	Truck, 3 ton, breakdown gantry, number 2, 3, 6x6	1941	3,622cc	V8
GMC	C60X	Truck, 3 ton, breakdown gantry, number 4, 6x6	1941	4,416cc	6
	Maple Leaf 1600	Truck, 3 ton, breakdown, LP3, 4x2	1940	4,416cc	6
Canada					
Chevrolet	C60L 8443	Truck, 3 ton, breakdown, 4x4	1942	3,540cc	6
	C60S 8442	Truck, 3 ton, breakdown, 4x4	1942	3,540cc	6
	1543	Truck, 3 ton, breakdown, 4x2	1943	3,540cc	6
Ford	EC098T	Truck, 3 ton, breakdown, 4x2	1940	3,917cc	V8
	F60L C298QF	Truck, 3 ton, breakdown, 4x4	1942	3,917cc	V8
	F60H C290QF	Truck, 3 ton, breakdown, 6x4	1940	3,867cc	V8
	F60H C010QF	Truck, 3 ton, breakdown gantry, 6x4	1940	3,917cc	V8
Germany					
Borgward	le.gl.E.Lkw	Truck, light, recovery, 6x6	1937	6,234cc	6 (D)
Büssing-NAG	4500A-1	Truck, heavy, recovery, 4x4	1942	7,412cc	6 (D)
	4500S-1	Truck, heavy, recovery, 4x2	1942	7,412cc	6 (D)
	le.gl.E.Lkw	Truck, light, recovery, 6x6	1937	6,234cc	6 (D)
Famo	F3	Tractor, heavy, crane, semi-track; SdKfz9	1939	10,838cc	V12
	F3	Tractor, heavy, 6 ton crane, semi-track; SdKfz9/1	1939	10,838cc	V12
	F3	Tractor, heavy, 10 ton crane, semi-track; SdKfz9/2	1939	10,838cc	V12
MAN	le.gl.E.Lkw	Truck, light, recovery, 6x6	1937	6,234cc	6 (D)
Great Britain					
Austin	K6/A	Truck, 3 ton, breakdown gantry, 6x4	1944	3,995cc	6
Crossley	30/70	Truck, 3 ton, breakdown, 6x4	1933	5,266cc	6
	FWD Type 1	Truck, 3 ton, breakdown, 4x4	1940	5,266cc	4
	IGL8	Truck, 3 ton, breakdown gantry, 6x4	1938	5,266cc	4
	Q Type	Truck, 3 ton, breakdown gantry, 4x4	1936	5,266cc	4
Ford	WOT6	Truck, 3 ton, breakdown gantry, 4x4	1942	3,621cc	V8
Guy	FBAX	Truck, 3 ton, breakdown gantry, 6x4	1938	5,112cc	6
Leyland	Retriever	Truck, 3 ton, breakdown gantry, 6x4	1938	5,895cc	6
Morris-Commercial	CDSW	Truck, 30cwt, light breakdown, 6x4	1938	3,485cc	6
Scammell	Pioneer SV/1T, 1S	Tractor, heavy breakdown, 6x4	1939	8,369cc	6 (D)
	Pioneer SV/2S	Tractor, heavy breakdown, 6x4	1939	8,369cc	6 (D)
Italy					
Breda	41	Tractor, heavy, recovery, 4x4	1941	8,850cc	6 (D)
Ceirano	47CM	Truck, medium, recovery, 4x2	1931	4,712cc	4

* V = cylinders in Vee formation; H = flat or horizontally-opposed configuration; (D) = diesel engine.

Make	Model	Description	Date	Engine: capacity	cylinders*
Japan					
Kokura or Sagami Arsenal	Ho-Fu	Recovery vehicle, full-track; Type 95	1941	n/a	n/a (D)
United States of America					
Autocar	C7066	Truck, 4 ton, wrecker, 6x6	1940	7,391cc	6
	U90	Truck, 5 ton, tractor, wrecking, 4x2	1940	8,210cc	6
Available Truck	-	Truck, medium wrecker, 6x4	1943	5,244cc	6
Biederman	-	Truck, 7½ ton, tractor, wrecking, Type C-2, 6x6	1939	12,766cc	6
Corbitt	-	Truck, 6 ton, heavy wrecker, 6x6; M1	1935	5,244cc	6
	54SD6	Truck, 7½ ton, tractor, wrecking, Type C-2, 6x6	1939	13,093cc	6
Diamond T	Model 967	Truck, 4 ton, wrecker, 6x6	1941	8,210cc	6
	Model 968A	Truck, 4 ton, wrecker, 6x6	1941	8,669cc	6
	Model 969, 969A	Truck, 4 ton, wrecker, 6x6	1941	8,669cc	6
Dodge-Thornton	T124 VK60, WK60	Truck, 3 ton, breakdown gantry, COE, 6x4	1940	5,424cc	6
Federal	605	Truck, 7½ ton, tractor, wrecking, Type C-2, 6x6	1940	14,011cc	6
	606	Truck, 7½ ton, tractor, wrecking, Type C-2, 6x6	1940	14,011cc	6
Ford	09W/MH	Truck, 1½ ton, wrecker, 4x4	1940	3,917cc	V8
	GTBB	Truck, 1½ ton, wrecker, 4x4	1943	3,703cc	6
GMC	ACK-352	Truck, 1½ ton, wrecker, 4x4	1940	4,064cc	6
	ACKWX-353	Truck, 2½ ton, wrecker, 6x6	1940	4,556cc	6
	CCKW-353	Truck, 2½ ton, light wrecker, number 7 set, 6x6	1941	4,416cc	6
International	M-5H-6	Truck, 2½ ton, light wrecker, 6x6	1941	5,211cc	6
Kenworth	570, 571, 572	Truck, 6 ton, heavy wrecker, 6x4; M1	1941	8,226cc	6
	573	Truck, heavy wrecker, 6x4; M1A1	1943	8,226cc	6
Mack	LMSW-23	Truck, 5 ton, wrecker, 6x4	1941	10,012cc	6
	LMSW-39	Truck, 5 ton, wrecker, 6x4	1942	10,012cc	6
	LMSW-53	Truck, 5 ton, wrecker, 6x4	1941	10,012cc	6
	LMSW-57	Truck, 5 ton, wrecker, 6x4	1943	10,012cc	6
Marmon-Herrington	TL 31-6	Truck, 6 ton, heavy wrecker, 6x6; M1	1935	5,244cc	6
Oshkosh	W709	Truck, 5 ton, wrecker, 4x4	1941	8,669cc	6
Reo	29XS	Truck, 7½ ton, tractor, wrecking, Type C-2, 6x6	1942	14,011cc	6
Sterling	DDS-235	Truck, 7½ ton, tractor, wrecking, Type C-2, 6x6	1942	12,766cc	6
	HCS-330	Truck, 15 ton, heavy wrecker, 6x4	1942	12,766cc	6
Ward LaFrance	Model 1000/1	Truck, 4 ton, wrecking, 6x6; M1	1940	8,226cc	6
	Model 1000/2	Truck, 6 ton, heavy wrecker, 6x6; M1	1942	7,571cc	6
	Model 1000/3, 4	Truck, 6 ton, heavy wrecker, 6x6; M1	1942	8,226cc	6
	Model 1000/5	Truck, 10 ton, heavy wrecker, 6x6; M1A1	1943	8,226cc	6
White	950X6	Truck, 4 ton, wrecker, 6x6	1940	5,932cc	6

* V = cylinders in Vee formation; H = flat or horizontally-opposed configuration; (D) = diesel engine.

Truck Mounted Cranes

Make	Model	Description	Date	Engine: capacity	cylinders*
Australia					
International	KS5	Truck, 3 ton, bomb crane, 4x2	1942	7,391cc	6
Canada					
Ford	F60S	Truck, 3 ton, derrick, 4x4	1940	3,917cc	V8
Germany					
Borgward	B3000S/D	Truck, medium, aircraft maintenance, 4x2	1938	4,962cc	6 (D)
Büssing-NAG	4500A-1	Truck, heavy, 3 ton crane, 4x4; Kfz96	1942	7,412cc	6 (D)
	4500S-1	Truck, heavy, 3 ton crane, 4x2; Kfz96	1942	7,412cc	6 (D)
	4500A-1	Truck, heavy, 5 ton crane, 4x4; Kfz96	1942	7,412cc	6 (D)
	4500S-1	Truck, heavy, 5 ton crane, 4x2; Kfz96	1942	7,412cc	6 (D)
Famo	F3	Tractor, heavy, 6 ton crane, semi-track; SdKfz9/1	1939	10,838cc	V12
	F3	Tractor, heavy, 10 ton crane, semi-track; SdKfz9/2	1939	10,838cc	V12
MAN	ML4500A	Truck, heavy, 3 ton crane, 4x4; Kfz96	1940	7,412cc	6 (D)
	ML4500S	Truck, heavy, 3 ton crane, 4x2; Kfz96	1940	7,980cc	6 (D)
	ML4500A	Truck, heavy, 5 ton crane, 4x4; Kfz96	1940	7,412cc	6 (D)
	ML4500S	Truck, heavy, 5 ton crane, 4x2; Kfz96	1940	7,980cc	6 (D)
Mercedes-Benz	L4500A	Truck, heavy, 3 ton crane, 4x4; Kfz96	1939	7,274cc	6 (D)
	L4500S	Truck, heavy, 3 ton crane, 4x2; Kfz96	1939	7,274cc	6 (D)
	L4500A	Truck, heavy, 5 ton crane, 4x4; Kfz96	1939	7,274cc	6 (D)
	L4500S	Truck, heavy, 5 ton crane, 4x2; Kfz96	1939	7,274cc	6 (D)
Great Britain					
AEC	Model O854	Truck, 5 ton, Coles 5 ton crane, 6x6	1942	7,781cc	6 (D)
Albion	AM463	Truck, 2 ton, Coles 2 ton crane, 4x2	1934	4,427cc	4
Austin	K6/ZB	Truck, 3 ton, Coles 2 ton crane, 6x4	1944	3,995cc	6
	K6/ZB	Truck, 3 ton, Coles 3 ton crane, 6x4	1944	3,995cc	6
Crossley	IGL8	Truck, 3 ton, Coles 2 ton crane, 6x4	1938	5,266cc	4
	IGL8	Truck, 3 ton, derrick, 6x4	1938	5,266cc	4
Guy	FBAX	Truck, 3 ton, derrick, 6x4	1938	5,112cc	4
Leyland	Retriever WLW3	Truck, 3 ton, Coles 2 ton crane, 6x4	1939	5,895cc	6
	Retriever WLW3	Truck, 3 ton, derrick, 6x4	1939	5,895cc	6
Thornycroft	Amazon WF8/NR6	Truck, 6 ton, Coles 5 ton crane, 6x4	1944	7,880cc	6 (D)
	Amazon WF8/AC6	Truck, 6 ton, Coles 5 ton crane, 6x4	1939	7,759cc	6
	Amazon WF/AC6	Truck, 6 ton, Coles 5 ton crane, 6x4	1939	7,759cc	6
	Amazon WF/AC6	Truck, 6 ton, Neales & Rapid 5 ton crane, 6x4	1940	7,759cc	6
United States of America					
Available Truck	CS-600(L)-SW	Truck, 10 ton, Harnischfeger or Link Belt crane, 6x4	1942	5,244cc	6
	CS-700(D)-SW	Truck, 10 ton, Harnischfeger or Link Belt crane, 6x4	1942	5,244cc	6
Bay City	18-T50	Truck, 4 ton, crane, 6x4	1942	n/a	6
Biederman	P1	Truck, 7½ ton, Michigan 10 ton crane, 6x6	1944	12,766cc	6

* V = cylinders in Vee formation; H = flat or horizontally-opposed configuration; (D) = diesel engine.

Make	Model	Description	Date	Engine: capacity	cylinders*
Brockway	B-666	Truck, 6 ton, bridge erector, 6x6	1942	14,011cc	6
	C-666	Truck, 6 ton, Quickway 4/8 ton crane, 6x6	1943	14,011cc	6
Caterpillar	D6	Tractor, medium, Cardwell 2 ton crane, full-track; M3	1941	7,669cc	6 (D)
	D7	Tractor, heavy, Cardwell 6 ton crane, full-track; M1	1940	13,618cc	4 (D)
Chevrolet	G-7128 NQ	Truck, 1½ ton, bomb service, 4x4; M6	1943	3,851cc	6
Colman	G55A	Truck, 4 ton, Quickway 4-8 ton crane, 4x4	1941	8,554cc	6
Corbitt	50SD6	Truck, 6 ton, Quickway 4-8 ton crane, 6x6	1944	14,011cc	6
Dart	200/353	Truck, 10 ton, Browning crane, 6x4	1941	12,766cc	6
	200/454-AWD	Truck, 10 ton, Browning crane, 6x6	1941	12,766cc	6
	300-AWD	Truck, 10 ton, Browning crane, 6x6	1942	12,766cc	6
	452-AWD	Truck, 10 ton, Bucyrus-Erie crane, 6x6	1942	12,766cc	6
Diamond T	Model 201	Truck, 1½ ton, bomb service, 4x2; M1	1941	3,867cc	6
	Model 968A	Truck, 4 ton, crane, swinging boom, 6x6; M1	1941	8,669cc	6
	Model 975, 975A	Truck, 4 ton, Bay City 4½ ton crane, 6x6	1941	8,669cc	6
	Model 975, 975A	Truck, 4 ton, Coles 3 ton crane, 6x6	1941	8,669cc	6
Ford	GTBS	Truck, 1½ ton, bomb service, 4x4	1942	3,703cc	6
	GTBC	Truck, 1½ ton, bomb service, 4x4	1943	3,703cc	6
Ford/Marmon	11Y/MH	Truck, ½ ton, bomb service, 4x2; M1	1941	3,622cc	V8
FWD	B-666	Truck, 6 ton, bridge erector, 6x6	1942	14,011cc	6
	C-666	Truck, 6 ton, Quickway 4-8 ton crane, 6x6	1944	14,011cc	6
GMC	AC-251	Truck, 1 ton, bomb service, 4x2; M1	1940	3,736cc	6
	CCKW-353	Truck, 2½ ton, bomb service, 6x6; M27	1941	4,416cc	6
Hendrickson	500B	Truck, 10 ton, Browning crane, 6x4	1944	n/a	n/a
International	-	Tractor, medium, Hughes 2 ton crane, full track; M3	1940	7,460cc	4 (D)
	-	Tractor, medium, Trackson 2 ton crane, full track; M5	1940	5,785cc	4
Mack	EG	Truck, 2½ ton, hoist and bucket, 4x2	1941	4,752cc	6
Thew Shovel	MC2	Truck, 10 ton, Moto-Crane 10-20 ton crane, 6x6; M2	1943	12,766cc	6
	MC3	Truck, 10 ton, Moto-Crane 10-20 ton crane, 6x6; M2	1943	12,766cc	6
	MC4	Truck, 10 ton, Moto-Crane 10-20 ton crane, 6x6; M2	1943	12,766cc	6
Ward LaFrance	B-666	Truck, 6 ton, bridge erector, 6x6	1942	14,011cc	6
White	B-666	Truck, 6 ton, bridge erector, 6x6	1942	14,011cc	6
	C-666	Truck, 6 ton, Quickway 4-8 ton crane, 6x6	1942	14,011cc	6

* V = cylinders in Vee formation; H = flat or horizontally-opposed configuration; (D) = diesel engine.

Fire Appliances and Snow Clearers

Make	Model	Description	Date	Engine: capacity	cylinders*
Germany					
Borgward	B3000A/D	Truck, medium, fire, 4x4; Kfz343, 344, 345, 346	1942	4,962cc	6 (D)
	B3000A/O	Truck, medium, fire, 4x4; Kfz343, 344, 345, 346	1942	3,745cc	6
	B3000S/O	Truck, medium, fire, 4x2; Kfz343, 344, 345, 346	1938	3,745cc	6
Büssing-NAG	le.gl.E.Lkw	Truck, light, turntable ladder, 6x6	1937	6,234cc	6 (D)
Henschel	le.gl.E.Lkw	Truck, light, turntable ladder, 6x6	1937	6,234cc	6 (D)
	33D1	Truck, medium, fire, 6x4; Kfz343, 344, 345, 346	1933	10,857cc	6
	33G1	Truck, medium, fire, 6x4; Kfz343, 344, 345, 346	1937	9,123cc	6 (D)
KHD	le.gl.E.Lkw	Truck, light, turntable ladder, 6x6	1937	6,234cc	6 (D)
	A3000	Truck, medium, fire, 4x4; Kfz343, 344, 345, 346	1941	4,942cc	4 (D)
	S3000	Truck, medium, fire, 4x2; Kfz343, 344, 345, 346	1941	4,942cc	4 (D)
Krupp	L3H63	Truck, medium, 6x4; Kfz343, 344, 345, 346	1931	7,542cc	6
	L3H163	Truck, medium, 6x4; Kfz343, 344, 345, 346	1936	7,542cc	6
Magirus	M206	Truck, light, fire crash, 6x4	1935	4,562cc	6
	33G1	Truck, medium, fire, 6x4; Kfz343, 344, 345, 346	1938	9,123cc	6 (D)
MAN	le.gl.E.Lkw	Truck, light, turntable ladder, 6x6	1937	6,234cc	6 (D)
	E3000	Truck, medium, fire, 4x2; Kfz343, 344, 345, 346	1940	4,503cc	4 (D)
Mercedes-Benz	le.gl.E.Lkw	Truck, light, turntable ladder, 6x6	1937	6,234cc	6 (D)
	L1500S	Truck, light, fire, 4x2; Kfz343, 344, 345, 346	1941	2,594cc	6
	L3000A	Truck, medium, fire, 4x4; Kfz343, 344, 345, 346	1939	4,849cc	4 (D)
	L3000S/O66	Truck, medium, fire, 4x2; Kfz343, 344, 345, 346	1940	4,849cc	4 (D)
	LG63/LG3000	Truck, medium, fire, 6x4; Kfz343, 344, 345, 346	1935	7,413cc	6 (D)
Opel	Blitz 3.6-36S	Truck, medium, fire, 4x2; Kfz343, 344, 345, 346	1937	3,626cc	6
	Blitz 3.6-6700A	Truck, medium, fire, 4x4; Kfz343, 344, 345, 346	1940	3,626cc	6
Great Britain					
Austin	K2/A	Truck, 2 ton, fire, auxiliary towing vehicle, 4x2	1940	3,462cc	6
	K2/A	Truck, 2 ton, fire tender, 4x2	1944	3,462cc	6
	K4	Truck, 3 ton, medium dam unit, 4x2	1941	3,995cc	6
	K4	Truck, 3 ton, escape, 4x2	1941	3,995cc	6
	K4	Truck, 3 ton, extra heavy pump, 1,100gpm, 4x2	1941	3,995cc	6
	K6	Truck, 3 ton, fire crash, CO_2, 6x4	1944	3,995cc	6
	K4	Truck, 3 ton, heavy pump, 700gpm, 4x2	1941	3,995cc	6
	K4	Truck, 3 ton, turntable ladder, 4x2	1941	3,995cc	6
Bedford	QLD	Truck, 3 ton, fire tender, 4x4	1943	3,519cc	6
	OY	Truck, 3 ton, extra heavy pump, 1,100gpm, 4x2	1939	3,519cc	6
Crossley	FE1	Truck, 3 ton, fire, foam/CO_2, 6x4	1938	5,266cc	4
	IGL8	Truck, 3 ton, fire tender, 6x4	1938	5,266cc	4
	Q Type	Truck, 3 ton, fire tender, 1,000gpm, 4x4	1936	5,266cc	4
Dodge ('Kew')	80B, 82, 82A	Truck, 3 ton, medium dam unit, 4x2	1940	5,420cc	6
Ford	WOT2H	Truck, 15 cwt, fire, auxiliary towing vehicle, 4x2	1940	3,621cc	V8
	7V	Truck, 3 ton, escape, 4x2	1940	3,621cc	V8
	7V	Truck, 3 ton, heavy pump, 700gpm, 4x2	1940	3,621cc	V8
	WOT1	Truck, 3 ton, fire crash, foam, 1,000gpm, 6x4	1942	3,621cc	V8
	WOT1A	Truck, 3 ton, fire crash, foam/CO_2, 6x4	1945	3,621cc	V8
	WOT1, WOT1A	Truck, 3 ton, fire crash, foam monitor, 6x4	1944	3,621cc	V8

* V = cylinders in Vee formation; H = flat or horizontally-opposed configuration; (D) = diesel engine.

Make	Model	Description	Date	Engine: capacity	cylinders*
Karrier	Bantam	Truck, 2 ton, fire tender, 4x2	1934	n/a	n/a
Leyland	Beaver	Truck, 3 ton, turntable ladder, 4x2	1940	n/a	6 (D)
	FKT	Truck, 3 ton, fire, 500gpm, 4x2	1939	7,642cc	6
Morris-Commercial	CVS	Truck, 3 ton, heavy pump, 700gpm, 4x2	1939	3,485cc	6

United States of America

Make	Model	Description	Date	Engine: capacity	cylinders*
American LaFrance	500 Series	Truck, fire, chemical/pumper, 750gpm, 4x2	1941	n/a	V12
	600 Series	Truck, fire, pumper, 1250gpm, 4x2	1942	n/a	V12
Brockway	B666	Truck, 6 ton, fire-crash, HP fog foam, 6x6	1942	14,011cc	6
Chevrolet	G7153	Truck, 1¹/₂ ton, fire, crash, COE, 4x4	1942	3,859cc	6
	G4112 ZP	Truck, 1¹/₂ ton, fire, crash, 4x4	1941	3,859cc	6
	G7103 NE	Truck, 1¹/₂ ton, fire, crash, 4x4	1942	3,859cc	6
	G7133 NZ	Truck, 1¹/₂ ton, fire, crash, 4x4	1942	3,859cc	6
	G7100	Truck, 1¹/₂ ton, fire, pumper, 300gpm, 4x4	1942	3,859cc	6
	MR	Truck, 1¹/₂ ton, fire, pumper, 300gpm/500gpm, 4x2	1942	3,859cc	6
Diamond T-Snogo	Model 968	Truck, 4 ton, snow plow, rotary, 6x6	1941	8,669cc	6
Dodge	RE31	Truck, 1¹/₂ ton, fire, pumper, 300gpm, 4x2	1940	3,949cc	6
Ford	2G8T	Truck, 1¹/₂ ton, fire, pumper, 300gpm, 4x2	1942	3,917cc	V8
	2G8T	Truck, 1¹/₂ ton, fire, pumper, 500gpm, 4x2	1941	3,917cc	V8
Ford-Snogo	2G8T	Truck, 1¹/₂ ton, snow plow, rotary, 4x1	1942	3,917cc	V8
Ford/Marmon	MM5-4	Truck, 1¹/₂ ton, fire, crash, 4x4	1941	3,917cc	V8
FWD-Snogo	HAR-1	Truck, 4 ton, snow plow, rotary, 4x4	1942	5,244cc	6
	SU-COE	Truck, 5-6 ton, snow plow, rotary, 4x4	1944	8,472cc	6
GMC	CCKW-353	Truck, 2¹/₂ ton, fire, pumper, 500gpm, 6x6	1941	4,416cc	6
Indian	MTC-18	Motor tricycle, fire, LP CO_2, 3x2	1941	1,206cc	V2
International	M-3L-4	Truck, 1¹/₂ ton, fire, crash, 4x4	1941	5,211cc	6
	K5	Truck, 2¹/₂ ton, fire, pumper, 300gpm, 4x2	1941	3,818cc	6
	M-5H-6	Truck, 2¹/₂ ton, fire, pumper, 750gpm, 6x6	1941	5,211cc	6
Kenworth	570	Truck, 6 ton, fire, crash, HP fog foam, 6x6	1941	8,226cc	6
Mack	EE	Truck, 1¹/₂ ton, fire, pumper, 500gpm, 4x2	1940	4,146cc	6
	19LS	Truck, 2¹/₂ ton, fire, pumper, 250gpm, 4x2	1943	8,357cc	6
	Type 75	Truck, 2¹/₂ ton, fire, pumper, 750gpm, 6x6	1942	8,357cc	6
	EHU	Truck, 5 ton, fire crash, COE, 4x2	1942	5,080cc	6
	NM3	Truck, 6 ton, fire, LP CO_2, 6x6	1942	11,586cc	6
	NN	Truck, 6 ton, fire, LP CO_2, 6x6	1941	11,586cc	6
Maxim Motors	-	Truck, fire, pumper, 750gpm, 4x2	1941	n/a	n/a
Oshkosh-Snogo	W700	Truck, 7¹/₂ ton, snow plow, rotary, 4x4	1943	8,669cc	6
Peter Pirsch	14	Truck, fire, pumper, 750gpm, 4x2	1940	9,144cc	6
	15	Truck, fire, pumper, 750gpm, 4x2	1940	9,144cc	6
Reo	27XFS	Truck, 7¹/₂ ton, fire, LP CO_2, 6x6	1943	14,011cc	6
	29FF	Truck, 7¹/₂ ton, fire, LP CO_2, 6x6	1943	14,011cc	6
Sterling	DDS-235	Truck, 7¹/₂ ton, fire, LP CO_2, 6x6	1943	12,766cc	6
Walter	FGBS	Truck, 8 ton, snow plow, speed and roto-wing, 4x4	1942	12,766cc	6
Ward LaFrance	B666	Truck, 6 ton, fire-crash, HP fog foam, Class 155, 6x6	1942	14,011cc	6

* V = cylinders in Vee formation; H = flat or horizontally-opposed configuration; (D) = diesel engine.

Amphibians

Make	Model	Description	Date	Engine: capacity	cylinders*
Germany					
Porsche	Type 128	Car, light, amphibian, 4x4	1940	985cc	H4
Sachsenberg	L-W-S	Tractor, full track, amphibian	1935	10,838cc	V12
Trippel	SG6/38	Car, medium, amphibian, 4x4	1938	2,473cc	6
	SG6/41	Car, medium, amphibian, 4x4	1941	2,473cc	6
	SG7	Car, medium, amphibian	1943	3,981cc	V8
Volkswagen	Type 166	Car, light, amphibian, 4x4; Kfz1/20	1942	1,131cc	H4
Great Britain					
Thornycroft	Terrapin Mk I	Truck, 4 ton, amphibian, 8x8	1943	7,242cc	2x V8
	Terrapin Mk II	Truck, 5 ton, amphibian, 8x8	1945	7,242cc	2x V8
Japan					
Toyota	KCY Su-Ki	Truck, 2 ton, amphibian, 4x4	1943	3,389cc	6
United States of America					
Amphibious Car	Aqua-Cheetah XAC	Truck, ½ ton, amphibian, 4x4	1942	3,772cc	6
Ford	GPA	Truck, ½ ton, amphibian, 4x4	1942	2,199cc	4
GMC	DUKW-353	Truck, 2½ ton, amphibian, 6x6	1942	4,416cc	6
Studebaker	Weasel	Carrier, light cargo, amphibian, full-track; M29C	1943	2,786cc	6

* V = cylinders in Vee formation; H = flat or horizontally-opposed configuration.

Right: The GMC amphibious DUKW was probably the best vehicle oif its type produced during the war. Consisting essentially of the engine, transmission and axles of the GM CCKW 2½-ton truck installed in a steel hull designed by Sparkman & Stevens, it was used to ferry supplies from ship to shore and was particularly useful following the Normandy landings when the Allies had yet to capture an intact port. *(IWM)*

Ambulances

Make	Model	Description	Date	Engine: capacity	cylinders*
Australia					
Ford	01T	Truck, 30cwt, ambulance, Indian Army type, 4x2	1940	3,622cc	V8
Chevrolet	1532	Truck, 30cwt, ambulance, Indian Army type, 4x2	1940	3,548cc	6
	1541	Truck, 30cwt, blood storage, 4x2	1941	3,548cc	6
	1500 Series	Truck, 3 ton, ambulance, 4x2	1940	3,548cc	6
	C60S	Truck, 3 ton, ambulance, 4x4	1940	3,548cc	6
Canada					
Chevrolet	C8A	Truck, 8cwt, ambulance, 4x4	1942	3,548cc	6
	C60L	Truck, 3 ton, ambulance, 4x4	1940	3,548cc	6
	C60L	Truck, 3 ton, dental surgery, 4x4	1940	3,548cc	6
	C60L	Truck, 3 ton, medical, 4x4	1940	3,548cc	6
	C60X	Truck, 3 ton, bacteriological laboratory, 6x6	1940	3,548cc	6
Ford	F30	Truck, 30cwt, ambulance, 4x4	1941	3,917cc	V8
	F60L	Truck, 3 ton, ambulance, 4x4	1940	3,917cc	V8
	F60H	Truck, 3 ton, X-ray, 6x6	1940	3,917cc	V8
Germany					
Adler	K-31 Diplomat	Car, medium, ambulance, 4x2	1938	2,916cc	6
BMW	326	Car, medium, medical, 4x2	1936	1,971cc	6
Ford	V8-51	Truck, medium, medical, 4x2	1936	3,600cc	V8
	V3000S/G197TS	Truck, medium, mobile surgical unit, 4x2	1939	3,600cc	V8
	V3000S/G198TS	Truck, medium, mobile surgical unit, 4x2	1941	3,900cc	V8

* V = cylinders in Vee formation; H = flat or horizontally-opposed configuration; (D) = diesel engine.

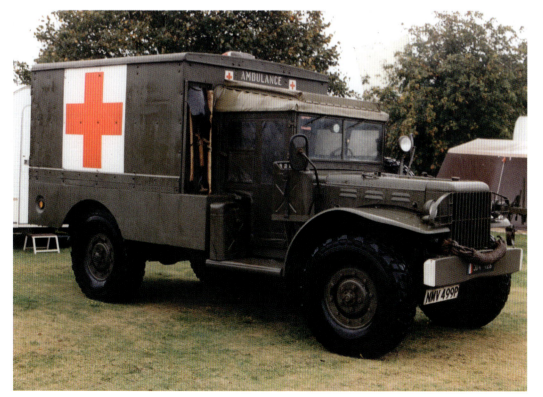

Left: In March 1944, the steel-bodied Dodge ³/₄-ton 4x4 WC54 ambulance was replaced by the WC64 'knock-down' - or KD - ambulance which could be reduced in height to simplify shipping. *(RG/TM)*

Make	Model	Description	Date	Engine: capacity	cylinders*
MAN	E3000	Truck, medium, mobile surgical unit, 4x2	1940	4,503cc	4 (D)
Horch	40; s.E.Pkw	Truck, light, ambulance, 4x4; Kfz31	1935	3,823cc	V8
Mercedes-Benz	L1100, LE1100	Truck, light, ambulance, 4x2; Kfz31	1938	n/a	4
	L1500E	Truck, light, ambulance, 4x2; Kfz31	1938	2,594cc	6
Opel	Blitz 2.5-32	Truck, light, ambulance, 4x2	1937	2,473cc	6
	Blitz 2.5-32	Truck, light, mobile surgical unit, 4x2	1937	2,473cc	6
	Blitz 3.6-6700A	Truck, medium, ambulance, 4x4	1940	3,626cc	6
Peugeot	202U	Truck, light, ambulance, 4x2 (French)	1939	1,133cc	4
	DK5J, D5A	Truck, 1.4 ton, ambulance, 4x2 (French)	1939	2,142cc	4
Phänomen	Granit 25H	Truck, light, ambulance, 4x4; Kfz31	1936	2,497cc	4
	Granit 1500A	Truck, light, ambulance, 4x4	1940	2,678cc	4
Skoda	256B	Truck, 2.5 ton, ambulance, 4x2 (Czech)	1939	3,138cc	6
Steyr	640/643	Truck, light, ambulance, 6x4 (Austrian)	1937	2,260cc	6

Great Britain

Make	Model	Description	Date	Engine: capacity	cylinders*
AEC	Regal O.662	Coach, 34 seat, ambulance, 4x2; Q Type	1938	8,800cc	6 (D)
	Regal O.662	Coach, 34 seat, dental surgery, 4x2; Q Type	1938	8,800cc	6 (D)
Albion	AM463	Truck, 30cwt, ambulance, 4x2	1934	4,427cc	4
	BY3	Truck, 3 ton, bacteriological laboratory, 6x4	1940	4,250cc	6
	KL127	Truck, 3 ton, X-ray laboratory, 6x4	1940	4,250cc	6
Austin	K2/Y	Truck, 2 ton, ambulance, 4x2	1940	3,462cc	6
Bedford	ML	Truck, 2 ton, ambulance, 4x2	1939	3,519cc	6
	OYC	Truck, 3 ton, X-ray laboratory, 4x2	1939	3,519cc	6
	QLC	Truck, 3 ton, dental surgery, 4x4	1941	3,519cc	6
	WTL	Truck, 3 ton, ambulance, 4x2	1934	3,519cc	6
Commer	Q3	Truck, 3 ton, ambulance, 4x2	1939	4,086cc	6
Ford	E88W	Truck, 25 cwt, ambulance, 4x2	1940	3,621cc	V8
	EO18T	Truck, 30cwt, ambulance, 4x2	1940	3,621cc	V8
	Thames 7V	Truck, 30cwt, ambulance, 4x2	1940	3,621cc	V8
	WOT1, WOT1A	Truck, 3 ton, ambulance, 6x4	1940	3,621cc	V8
	WOT1, WOT1A	Truck, 3 ton, dental surgery, 6x4	1940	3,621cc	V8
Humber	FWD	Truck, 8 cwt, ambulance, light, 4x4	1940	4,086cc	6
Morris	TWV Series III	Ambulance, light, 4x2	1935	1,292cc	4
	Y14	Ambulance, light, 4x2	1936	1,818cc	6
Morris-Commercial	CS8	Truck, 15cwt, ambulance, 4x2	1934	3,485cc	6
	CD	Truck, 30cwt, ambulance, 4x2	1933	3,519cc	4
	CDF	Truck, 30cwt, ambulance, 6x4	1934	3,519cc	4
	CS11/30F	Truck, 30cwt, ambulance, 4x2	1935	3,485cc	6
Standard	14	Ambulance, light, 4x2	1936	1,776cc	4

Italy

Make	Model	Description	Date	Engine: capacity	cylinders*
Fiat	618M 'Col'	Truck, light, 1,300kg, ambulance, 4x2	1934	1,944cc	4
SPA	38RA	Truck, medium, ambulance, 4x2	1936	4,053cc	4

* V = cylinders in Vee formation; H = flat or horizontally-opposed configuration; (D) = diesel engine.

Make	Model	Description	Date	Engine: capacity	cylinders*
Japan					
Isuzu	Type 94A	Truck, 1$^{1}/_{2}$ ton, ambulance, 4x2	1934	4,390cc	6
	Type 94A	Truck, 1$^{1}/_{2}$ ton, ambulance, 6x4	1934	4,390cc	6
	Type 94B	Truck, 1$^{1}/_{2}$ ton, ambulance, 6x4	1934	4,840cc	4 (D)
Soviet Union					
GAZ	05-193	Truck, 1$^{1}/_{2}$ ton, ambulance, 6x4	1936	3,285cc	4
	55	Truck, 1$^{1}/_{2}$ ton, ambulance, 4x2	1938	3,285cc	4
United States of America					
Cadillac-Superior	62	Ambulance, 1/2 ton, metropolitan, 4 stretcher, 4x2	1941	5,670cc	V8
Chevrolet	WA	Truck, 1$^{1}/_{2}$ ton, field ambulance, 4x2	1940	3,548cc	6
	YR	Truck, 1$^{1}/_{2}$ ton, field ambulance, 4x2	1941	3,548cc	6
	MR	Truck, 1$^{1}/_{2}$ ton, ambulance, 4x2	1940	3,540cc	6
	WA	Truck, 1$^{1}/_{2}$ ton, ambulance, 4x2	1940	3,540cc	6
Dodge	T211-WC18	Truck, $^{1}/_{2}$ ton, ambulance, 4x4	1941	3,572cc	6
	T207-WC9	Truck, $^{1}/_{2}$ ton, ambulance, 4x4	1941	3,572cc	6
	T215-WC27	Truck, $^{1}/_{2}$ ton, ambulance, 4x4	1941	3,772cc	6
	T214-WC54	Truck, $^{1}/_{2}$ ton, ambulance, 4x4	1942	3,772cc	6
	T214-WC64	Truck, $^{1}/_{2}$ ton, ambulance, KD, 4x4	1944	3,772cc	6
	T203-VF407	Truck, 1$^{1}/_{2}$ ton, ambulance, 4x4	1940	3,299cc	6
GMC	CCKW-353	Truck, 2$^{1}/_{2}$ ton, special ambulance, 6x6	1941	4,416cc	6
	CCKW-353	Truck, 2$^{1}/_{2}$ ton, mobile surgical unit, 6x6	1941	4,416cc	6
	CCKW-353	Truck, 2$^{1}/_{2}$ ton, dental surgery, 6x6	1941	4,416cc	6
International	M-1-4	Truck, $^{1}/_{2}$ ton, ambulance, 4x4	1941	3,818cc	6
LaSalle	4-50	Ambulance, $^{1}/_{2}$ ton, metropolitan, 4 stretcher, 4x2	1944	5,277cc	V8
Linn Coach	-	Truck, 1$^{1}/_{2}$ ton, mobile surgical unit, 4x2	1940	3,622cc	V8
	-	Ambulance, 1$^{1}/_{2}$ ton, metropolitan, 12 stretcher, 4x2	1945	3,772cc	6
Packard-Henney	4194-HDA	Ambulance, $^{1}/_{2}$ ton, metropolitan, 4 stretcher, 4x2	1941	4,621cc	8
	4294-HDA	Ambulance, $^{1}/_{2}$ ton, metropolitan, 4 stretcher, 4x2	1942	4,621cc	8

* V = cylinders in Vee formation; H = flat or horizontally-opposed configuration; (D) = diesel engine.

Above: Approximately 52,000 examples of the standardised VW Type 82 *Kübelwagen* were produced between 1939 and 1945. *(UB)*